Robert Burns

Burns' Merry Muses

a choice collection of the favorite Scot's songs selected for the use of the

Crohallan fencibles

Robert Burns

Burns' Merry Muses
a choice collection of the favorite Scot's songs selected for the use of the Crohallan fencibles

ISBN/EAN: 9783337266066

Printed in Europe, USA, Canada, Australia, Japan

Cover: Foto ©Thomas Meinert / pixelio.de

More available books at **www.hansebooks.com**

Burns' Merry Muses

A CHOICE COLLECTION

OF

Favourite Songs.

Say, Puritan, can it be wrong,
To dress plain truth in witty song?
What honest Nature says we should do;
What ev'ry lady does,—or would do.

PRINTED FOR PRIVATE CIRCULATION.

EDINBURGH:
1886.

INDEX OF CONTENTS.

A

	PAGE.
As I came o'er the Cairney mount,	19
As honest Jacob on a night,	27
Altho' my back be at the wa',	29
As Sylvia on her arm reclining,	50
As a crab-louse and flea were ahunting together,	67
A beautiful lady, in fair London town,	75
A lovely lass to a friar came,	82

B

Blythe, blythe, blythe was she,	52
Beneath a weeping willow's shade,	114
Brimful of love fat Lydy sat,	115

C

Comin' o'er the hills o' Coupar,	38
Come prick up your ears and attend, sirs, awhile,	98

D

	PAGE.
Dinner o'er and grace said,	4
Duncan Macleerie, and Janet, his wife,	45
Disguis'd last night, I rush'd from home,	104

F

For London, when with fav'ring gale,	72

G

Gudewife, when your gudeman's frae hame,	25
Gat ye me, O gat ye me,	53

I

I once was a maid, tho' I cannot tell when,	20
I rede ye beware o' the ripples, young man,	30
In Edinbrugh town they've made a law,	31
I'll tell ye a tale o' a wife,	36
I, a tender young maid,	79
I wonder, quoth dame, as her spouse she embraces,	90
I'll trip upon trenchers, I'll dance upon dishes,	94
I can't for my life guess the cause of this fuss,	116
I sing the British fair one's charms,	119

J

Jenny sits up i' the laft,	39
John Thompson keekit in at the keyhole,	94

L

	PAGE.
Let the philosophic wise,	58
Let him, fond of fibbing,	87

M

My auntie Jean held to the shore,	24
My Sally is the blythest maid,	70
Maggy lives on yon ha' head,	73

N

Not far from town, a country squire,	47
Nancy, on a sofa lying,	66

O

O! saw ye my Maggy,	2
O yon, yon, yon lassie,	17
O wha my baby clouts will buy,	18
O ere yestreen I stented graith,	22
O Errock stane, may never maid,	23
Our bride flate, an' our bride flang,	41
O wha'll kiss me now, my Jo,	42
O will ye speak at our town,	43
One winter's night, in am'rous mood,	49
O can ye labour lee, young man,	54

	PAGE.
O gie the lass her fairin', lad,	56
One day at her toilet, as Venus began,	89
O lassie, art thou sleeping yet,	93

P

Put butter in my Donald's brose,	26
Puff'd up wi' pride, (that's sure to fall,)	60
Papilio, the rich, in the hurry of love,	102

R

Roseberry to his lady says,	11

T

The modiewark has done me ill,	10
The ploughman he's a bonie lad,	12
The bonie lass o' Liviston,	32
There liv'd a lady in Lauderdale,	33
There liv'd a wife in Whistlecockpen,	35
There was a lass, they ca'd her Meg,	46
They took me to the haly band,	47
Twa neebour wives sat i' the sun,	55
There cam a cadger out o' Fife,	58
'Twas on a sweet May morning,	63
The boniest lass that ye meet neist,	92
The marriage morn I can't forget,	100
The night her silent sable wore,	105

	PAGE
The taylor came to clout the claise,	107
The maid's gane to the mill by night,	109
The coach arriv'd, impatient all,	112

W

When princes and prelates,	7
Whilst others to thy bosom rise,	14
When maukin bucks at early ——,	40
We'll hide the cooper behind the door,	57
When Fanny, blooming fair,	83
Whenever Chloe, I begin,	84
Who has e'er been at Holborn,	121

Y

Yestreen I had a pint o' wine,	1
You jovial boys, who love the joys,	9
Ye coopers and hoopers, attend to my ditty,	18
Ye hae lain wrang, lassie,	34
Ye botanists yield, I've discovered a root,	62
Ye delicate lovelies, with leave, I maintain,	85
Ye sons of Anacreon, assist me in song,	97

ANNA.

Tune—*The Banks of Banna.*

Yestreen I had a pint o' wine,
   A place where body saw na';
Yestreen lay on this breast o' mine,
   The raven locks of Anna:
The hungry Jew, in wilderness,
   Rejoicing o'er his manna,
Was naething to my hinny bliss,
   Upon the lips of Anna.

Ye monarchs tak' the East and west,
   Frae Indus to Savannah;
Gie me within my straining grasp,
   The melting form of Anna:
Then I'll despise imperial charms,
   An empress or sultana;
While dying raptures, in her arms,
   I give an' take with Anna.

Awa thou flaunting God of Day!
 Awa thou pale Diana!
Ilk starn gae hide thy twinkling ray
 When I'm to meet my Anna.
Come in thy raven plumage, Night,
 Sun, moon, and stars withdrawn a'!
An' bring an angel-pen, to write
 My transports wi' my Anna.

POSTSCRIPT.

The kirk and state may join an' tell;
 To do sic things I manna:
The kirk an' state may gae to h-l,
 An' I'll gae to my Anna.
She is the sunshine o' my e'e,
 To live but her I canna;
Had I on earth but wishes three,
 The first should be my Anna.

O, SAW YE MY MAGGY.

TUNE—*Saw Ye Na My Peggy.*

O saw ye my Maggy,
O saw ye my Maggy,
O saw ye my Maggy,
 Comin' o'er the lee?

What mark has your Maggy,
What mark has your Maggy,
What mark has your Maggy,
   That ane may ken her be?
My Maggy has a mark,
You'll find it in the dark;
It's in below her sark,
   A little aboon her knee.

What wealth has your Maggy,
What wealth has your Maggy,
What wealth has your Maggy,
   In tocher, gear, or fee?
My Maggy has a treasure,
A hidden mine o' pleasure,
I'll howk it at my leisure,
   It's a' alane for me.

How meet ye your Maggy,
How meet ye your Maggy,
How meet ye your Maggy,
   When nane's to hear or see?
E'en that tell our wishes,
Eager glowing kisses,
Then diviner blisses,
   In holy ecstacy!

How looe ye your Maggy,
How looe ye your Maggy,
How looe ye your Maggy,
  And looe nane but she?
Heav'nly joys before me!
Rapture trembling o'er me!
Maggy, I adore thee
  On my bended knee.

THE TOASTS.

Dinner o'er, and grace said, we'll for bus'ness prepare,
Arrang'd right and left in support of the chair;
We'll chorus the song as the circling toast passes,
And manage our bumpers as musical glasses.

To your lips, my convivials, the burgundy lift,
May we never want courage when put to the shift;
Here's what tars dislike, and lassies like best;
What's that? you may whisper; why, 'tis to be prest.

Ye fowlers, who eager at partridges aim,
Don't mark the maim'd covey, but mind better game;
'Tis beauty's the sport to repay sportsmen's trouble,
And there may your pointers stand stiff in the stubble.

To game we give laws, and game laws we have skill in:
Here's love's laws, and they who those laws are fulfillin';

But never may damsels demur to our sport,
Nor we suffer non-suits when call'd into court.

Like the Indians when warring, our game we must flush,
On our breasts as we lie, we present thro' the bush;
Here's the nest in that bush, and the bird-nesting lover;
Here's Middlesex bush-fighting, rest and recover.

Asthmatical lovers exist but to eat;
They purchase repletions at each turtle treat;
Our feasts boast a flavour, unknown to made dishes;
Here's life's dainty, dressed up with the sweet sauce of kisses.

Fair befall ev'ry lass, fair may fine ladies fall,
No colour I'll fix on, but drink to them all:
The black, the brunette, and the golden-lock'd dame,
The lock of all lock, and unlocking the same.

More upright foreknowledge that lock is commanding,
Than all other locks, or Locke's Understanding;
That lock has the casket of Cupid within it:
So here's to the key, lads—the critical minute.

Lads, pour forth libations from bottles and bowls:
The mother of all-saints should be drunk by all souls;

Here's to the downbed of beauty, which upraises man,
And beneath the thatc'd house, the miraculous cann.

Here's the dockyard that furnishes Great Britain's fleets,
The bookbinder's wife manufacturing in sheets;
The brown female reaper, who dares undertake her,
And the wife of Will Wattle, the neat basker-maker.

Here's Beersheba's cockpit, where David stood sentry;
Eve's custom-house, where Adam made the first entry;
Here's the pleasant-plac'd waterfall 'midst Bushy park;
The nick makes the tail stand, the farrier's wife's mark.

That the hungry be filled with rich things, let us say,
And well pleas'd may the rich be sent empty away;
Here's the miller's wife's music; the lass that's lamb-like,
And the fence of the farmer, on the top of love's dyke.

But why from this roundabout phrase must be guess'd,
What in one single syllable's better express'd;
That syllable, then, I my sentiment call,
So here's to the word which is one word for all.

POOR BODIES DO NAETHING BUT M—W.

TUNE—*The Campbells are Comin'*.

When princes and prelates,
An' hot-headed zealates,
A' Europe had set in a low, a low;
The poor man lies down,
Nor envies a crown,
But comforts himsel' wi' a m-w, a m-w.

An' why shou'd na poor bodies m-w, m-w, m-w,
An' why shou'd na poor bodies m-w;
The rich then hae siller, an' houses, an' land,
Poor bodies hae naething but m-w.

When P—s—k's great prince
Gade a cruizin to France,
Republican billies to cow, cow, cow;
Great B—s—k's strang prince
Wadda shawn better sense,
At hame wi' his prin—ss to m-w, m-w, m-w.

An' why, &c.

The E—b—r swore,
By sea an' by shore,
At Paris to kick up a row, a row;

But Paris, ay ready,
Just leugh at the laddie,
An' bade him gae hame, an' gae m-w, mw, m-w.

  An' why, &c.

When the brave duke of Y—k,
The Rhine first did pass,
Republican armies to cow, cow, cow,
They bade him gae hame,
To his P—ss—n dame,
An' gie her a kiss an' a m-w, a m-w.

  An' why, &c.

But over the Rhine,
Proud P——ss-a did shine,
To spend his last bluid he did vow, vow, vow;
But F—d——ck had better
Ne'er forded the water,
But spent as he dought at a m-w, a m-w.

  An' why, &c.

The black-headed eagle,
As keen as a beagle,
He hunted o'er height an' o'er howe, howe, howe;
In the braes of Gemap,
He fell in a trap,
E'en let him come out as he dow, dow, dow.

  Ah' why, &c.

Then fill up your glasses,
  Ye sons 'o Parnassus,
This toast I'am sure you'll allow, allow;
  Here's Geordie our king,
  And Charlotte his queen,
And lang may they live for to m-w, m-w, m-w.
  An' why, &c.

THE FORNICATOR.

Tune—*Clout the Cauldron.*

You jovial boys, who love the joys,
  The blessfu' joys of lovers;
An' dare avow't wi' dauntless brow,
  Whate'er the lass discovers;
I pray draw near, an' you shall hear,
  An' welcome in a *frater*,
I've lately been on quarantine,
  A proven fornicator.

Before the congregation wide,
  I past the muster fairly;
My handsome Betsey by my side,
  We gat our ditty rarely.
My downcast eye, by chance did spy,
  What made my mouth to water,

Those limbs sae clean, where I between,
    Commenced fornicator.

Wi' ruefu' face an' signs o' grace,
    I paid the buttock hire;
The night was dark, an' thro' the park,
    I cou'dna but convoy her.
A parting kiss, what cou'd I less,
    My vows becan to scatter;
Sweet Betsey fell, fal lal de ral;
    I am a fornicator.

But, by the sun an' moon I swear,
    An' I'll fulfil ilk hair o't,
That while I own a single crown,
    She's welcome to a share o't.
My roguish boy, his mother's joy,
    An' darling of his *pater*,
I for his sake the name will take,
    A harden'd fornicator.

THE MODIEWARK.

TUNE—*O For Ane an' Twenty Tam.*

The modiewark has done me ill,
An' below my apron has biggit a hill;
I maun consult some learned clark
About this wanton modiewark.

An' o the wanton modiewark;
The weary wanton modiewark;
I maun consult some learned clark,
About this wanton modiewark.

O first it gat between my taes,
Out o'er my garter niest it gaes;
At lenght it crap below my sark,
The weary wanton modiewark.
    An' o, &c.

This modiewark, tho' it be blin',
If ance the nose o't you lat in,
Then to the hilts, within a crack,
Its out o' sight, the modiewark.
    An' o, &c.

When Marjorie was made a bride,
An' Willy lay down by her side;
Syne nocht was hard, when a' was dark,
But kicking at the modiewark.
    An' o, &c.

SUPPER IS NA READY.

TUNE—*Clout the Cauldron.*

Roseberry to his lady says,
"My hinnie and my succor,

"O shall we do the thing you ken?
"Or shall we take our supper?"

Fal, lal, &c.

Wi' modest face, sae fu' o' grace,
  Reply'd the bonnie lady,
"My noble lord, do as ye please,
"But supper is na ready."

Fal, lal, &c.

THE PLOUGHMAN.

The ploughman he's a bonnie lad,
  His mind is ever true, Jo;
His garters knit below his knee,
  His bonnet it is blue, Jo.

 Sing up wi't a', the ploughman lad,
 And hey the merry ploughman;
 O' a' the trades that I do ken,
 Commend me to the ploughman.

As wakin' forth upon a day,
  I met a jolly ploughman;
I told him I had lands to plough,
  If that he wad prove true, man.

 Sing, &c.

He says, my dear, tak ye nae fear,
　　I'll fit you till a hair, Jo;
I'll cleave it up, and hit it down,
　　And water-furrow't fair, Jo.
　　　　Sing, &c.

I hae three ousen in my pleugh,
　　Three better ne'r plough'd ground, Jo,
The formost ox is plump and sma',
　　The twa are plump and round, Jo.
　　　　Sing, &c.

Then he wi' speed did yoke his pleugh,
　　Which by a gaud was driven, Jo;
But when he was atween the stilts,
　　I thought I was in heaven, Jo.
　　　　Sing, &c.

But the foremost ox fell in the fur,
　　The tither two did founder;
The ploughman lad he breathless grew,
　　In trowth, it was nae wonder.
　　　　Sing, &c.

But a sykie risk, below a hill,
　　The plough she took a stane, Jo,

Which gart the fire flee frae the sock,
The plowman gied a grane, Jo.
  Sing, &c.

I hae plough'd east, I hae plough'd west,
In weather foul and fair, Jo;
But the fairest ploughing e'er I plough'd,
Was ploughing amang hair, Jo.
  Sing, &c.

Sing up wi'd a', and in wi't a',
And hey my merry ploughman;
O' a' the trades and crafts I ken,
Commend me to the ploughman.
  Sing, &c.

THE BOWER OF BLISS.

  Tune—*Logan Water.*

Whilst others to thy bosom rise,
And paint the glories of thine eyes,
Or bid thy lips and cheeks disclose,
The unfading bloom of Eden's rose;
Less obvious charms my song inspire,
Which felt, not fear'd, we most admire,
Less obvious charms, not less divine,
I sing that lovely bower of thine.

Rich gems worth India's wealth alone,
How much pursued, how little known;
Tho' rough its face, tho' dim its hue,
It foils the lustre of Peru.
The vet'ran such a prize to gain,
Might all the toils of war sustain;
The devotee forsakes his shrine,
To venerate that bower of thine.

When the stung heart feels keen desire,
And thro' each vein pours liquid fire;
When, with flush'd cheeks and burning eyes,
Thy lover to thy bosom flies;
Believe, dear maid, believe my vow,
By Venus' self, I swear, tis true;
More bright thy higher beauties shine,
Illum'd by that strange bower of thine.

What thought sublime, what lofty strain,
Its wondrous virtues can explain?
No place, howe'er remote, can be
From its intense attraction free;
Tho' more elastic far than steel,
Its force ten thousand needles feel;
Pleas'd their high temper to resign,
In that magnetic bower of thine.

Irriguous vale, embrown'd with shades
Which no obtrusive storm pervades;
Soft clime, where native summer glows,
And nectar'd living current flows!
Not Tempe's vale, renowned of yore,
Of charms could boast such endless store;
More than elysian sweets combine
To grace that smiling bower of thine.

O! may no rash invaders stain,
Love's warm sequester'd virgin fane!
For me alone let gentle fate
Preserve the dear august retreat!
Along its banks when shall I sray?
Its beauteous landscape when survey?
How long in fruitless anguish pine?
Nor view unveil'd that bower of thine.

O! let my tender, trembling hand,
The awful gate of life expand!
With all its wonders feast my sight;
Dear prelude to immense delight!
Till plung'd in liquid joy profound,
The dark unfathom'd deep I sound;
All panting on thy breast recline,
And, murmuring, bless that bower of thine.

YON, YON, YON LASSIE.

Tune—*Ruffian's Rant.*

O yon, yon, yon lassie,
  Yon, yon, yon;
I never met a bonie lassie,
  But what wad play at you.

    O yon, yon, &c.

I never saw a silken gown,
  But I wad kiss the sleeve o't;
I never saw a maidenhead,
  That I wad spier the leave o't.

    O yon, yon, &c.

Tell nae me o' Meg my wife,
  That crowdie has nae savour;
But gie to me a bonie lass,
  An' let me steal the favour.

    O yon, yon, &c.

Gie me her I kis't yestreen,
  I vow but she was handsome,
For ilka briss upon her ——,
  Was worth a royal ransom.

    An' yon, yon, yon lassie,
      Yon, yon, yon;
    I never saw a bonie lass,
      But what wad play at you.

THE RANTIN' DOG, THE DADDIE O'T.

Tune—*East Nook o' Fife.*

O wha my babie clouts will buy?
O wha will tent me when I cry?
O wha will kiss me whare I lie,
    But the rantin' dog, the daddie o't?
O wha will own he did the faut?
O wha will buy the groanin' maut?
O wha will tell me how to ca't,
    But the rantin' dog, the daddie o't?

An' when I mount the creepie chair,
O wha will sit beside me there?
Just gie me Rab, I ask nae mair,
    But the rantin' dog, the daddie o't.
O wha will crack to me my lane?
An' wha will mak me fidgin' fain?
O wha will kiss me o'er again,
    But the rantin' dog, the daddie o't?

THE COOPER O' DUNDEE.

Tune—*Bonny Dundee.*

Ye coopers and hoopers attend to my ditty,
  I sing o' a cooper wha dwelt in Dundee;
This young man he was baith am'rous and witty,
  He pleas'd the fair maids wi' a blink o' his ee.

He was nae a cooper, a common tub-hooper,
   The most o' his trade lay in pleasin' the fair;
He hoop't them, he coop't them, he bor't them, he plug't them,
   An' a' sent for sandie when out o' repair.

For a twelvemonth or sae this youth was respectit,
   An' he was as busie as weel he could be;
But his bis'ness increas'd sae, that some were neglectit,
   Which ruin'd his trade in the town o' Dundee.

A baillie's fair daughter had wanted a coopin',
   And sandie was sent for, as oft times was he;
He yerk'd her sae hard, that she sprung an end-hoopin',
   Which banis'd poor sandie frae bonny Dundee.

THE HIGHLAND LADDIE.

As I cam o'r the Cairney mount,
   Down amang the blooming heather,
The highland laddie drew his durk,
   And sheath'd it in my wanton leather.

O my bonnie, bonnie highland laddie,
   My handsome, charming highland laddie.
When I am sick and like to die,
   He'll row me in his highland pladdie.

With me he played his warlike pranks,
    And on me boldly did adventure,
He did attack me on both the flanks,
    And push'd me fiercely in the centre.
        O my bonnie, &c.

A furious feight he did maintain,
    Wi' equal courage and desire;
Altho' he charg'd me three to ane,
    I stood my ground, and receiv'd his fire.
        O my bonnie, &c.

But our ammunition being spent,
    And we quite out o' breath an' sweating,
We did agree, wi' ae consent,
    To feight it out at the next meeting.
        O my bonnie, etc.

SOGER LADDIE.

I once was a maid, tho' I canna tell when,
An' still my delight is in proper young men;
Some one of a troop of gragoons was my daddie,
No wonder I'm fond of a soger laddie.
        Sing, lal de lal, &c.

The first of my lovers was a swagg'rin' blade,
To rattle the thundering drum was his trade;
His leg was so tight, and his cheek was so ruddy,
Transported I was with my soger laddie.

  Sing, lal de lal, &c.

But the godly old chaplain left him in the lurch,
The sword I forsook for the sake of the church;
He ventur'd the *soul*, and I risk'd the *body*,
'Twas then I prov'd false to my soger laddie.

  Sing, lal de lal, &c.

Full soon I grew sick of my sanctified sot,
The regiment at large for a husband I got;
From the gilded spontoon to the fife I was read,
I asked no more but a soger laddie.

  Sing, lal de lal, &c.

But the peace it reduc'd me to beg in despair,
Till I met my old laddie at Quinnigham fair;
His *rags regimental* they flutter'd so gaudy,
My heart it rejoic'd at my soger laddie.

  Sing, lal de lal, &c.

An' now I have liv'd—I know not how long,
An' still I can joy in a cup or a song;
And whilst with both hands I can hold the glass steady,
Here's to thee, my hero, my soger laddie.

  Sing, lal de lal, &c.

THERE'S HAIR ON'T.

Tune—*Push About the Jorum.*

O ere yestreen I stented graith,
    An' labour'd lang an' sair on't;
But fient a work, nor work wad it,
    There's sic a crap o' hair on't.

    There's hair on't, there's hair on't,
        There's thretty thrave an' mair on't;
    But gin I live t'anither year,
        I'll tether my grey naigs on't.

An' up the glen there was a knowe,
    Below the knowe a lair on't;
I maist had perish'd fit an' horse,
    I cou'd na see for hair on't.
        There's hair on't, &c.

But I'll plant a stake into the flowe,
    That ploughman may take care on't;
An' lay twa steppin' stanes below,
    An' syne I'll cowe the hair on't.
        There's hair on't, &c.

ERROCK BRAE.

Tune—*Sir Alex. Don's Strathspey.*

O Errock stane, may never maid
  A maiden by these gae,
Nor e'er a stane o' stan'in' graith,
  Gae stan'in' o'er the brae.

    An' tillin' Errock brae, young man,
      An' tillin' Errock brae;
    An open fur, an' stan'in' graith,
      Maun till the Errock brae.

As I sat by the Errock stane,
  Surveyin' far an' near,
Up cam a Cameronian
  Wi' a' his preachin' gear.
    An' tillin', &c.

He flang the bible o'er the brae,
  Amang the rashy gerse,
But the solemn league an' covenant
  He laid below my ——.
    An' tillin', &c.

An' on the edge o' Errock brae,
  He gae me sic a sten,

That o'er, an o'er, an' o'er we row'd,
    Till we cam to the glen.
        An' tillin', &c.

Yet still his —— held the grip,
    An' still his —— hang,
That a synod cou'dna tell the a-se,
    To wham they did belang.
        An' tillin', &c.

A prelate he loups on before,
    A Catholic behin';
But gie me a Cameronian,
    He'll m-w a body blin'.
        An' tillin', &c.

MY AUNTIE JEANIE'S BED.

        TUNE—*John Anderson.*

My auntie Jean held to the shore,
    As Ailsa boats cam back,
An' she has coft a feather-bed
    For twenty au' a plack;
An' in't she wan guid fifty mark,
    Before a towmond sped;
O! what a noble bargain
    Was auntie Jeannie's bed!

WAD YE DO THAT.

Same Tune.

Gudewife, when your gudeman's frae hame,
    Might I but be sae bauld,
As come to your bed-chamber,
    When winter nights are cauld?
As come to your bed-chamber,
    When nights are cauld an' wat;
An' lie in your gudeman's stead,
    Gudewife, wad ye do do that?

Young man, gif ye should be sae kind,
    When our gudeman's frae hame,
As come to my bed-chamber,
    Whare I am laid my lane,
An' lie in our gudeman's stead;
    I will tell you what,
He ——— me five times ikla night,
    Young man, wad ye do that?

FOR A' THAT, AN' A' THAT.

Put butter in my Donald's brose,
  For weel does Donald fa' that;
I loe my Donald's tartans weel,
  His naked a-se, an' a' that.

  For a' that, an' a' that,
    An' twice as meikle's a' that,
  The lassie gat a skelpit doup,
    But wan the day, for a' that.

For Donald sware a solemn aith,
  By his first hairy gravat!
That he wad fight the battle there,
  An' stick the lass, an' a' that.
    For a' that, &c.

His ——, baith side an' wide,
  Hang like a beggar's wallet;
An' ——, like a rollin'-pin,
  She nicher'd when she saw that.
    For a' that, &c.

Then she turn'd up her —— ——,
  An' she bade Donald claw that;
The deevil's dizzen Donald drew,
  An' Donald gied her a' that.

An' a' that, an' a' that,
   An' twice as meikle's a' that;
The lassie gat a skelpit doup,
   But wan the day, for a' that.

THE PATRIARCH.

Tune—*The Auld Cripple Dow.*

As honest Jacob on a night,
   Wi' his beloved beauty,
Was duly laid on wedlock's bed,
   An' noddin at his duty.

   Fal de lal, &c.

"How lang," she says, "ye fumblin' wretch,
   "Will ye be ——— at it?
"My eldest wean might die o' age,
   "Before that you could get it.

"Ye pech, an' grane, an' groazle there,
   "An mak an unco splutter,
"An' I maun lie an' thole you her,
   "An' fient ae hair the better."

Then he, in wrath, put up his graith,
   "The deevil's in the hissie!

"I m-w you as I m-w the lave,
"An' night an' day I'm bizzy.

"I've bairn'd the servant gypsies baith,
"Forbye your titty Leah;
"Ye barren jad, ye pit me mad,
"What mair can I do wi' you.

"There's ne'er a m-w I've gien the lave,
"But ye ha'e got a dizzen;
"An' —— a ane ye'se get again,
"Altho' your —— should gizzen."

But Rachel, calm as any lamb,
  She claps him on the waulies,
Quo' she, "Ne'er fash a woman's clash,
"In troth, ye m-w my brawlies.

"My dear, 'tis true, for many a m-w,
"I'm your ungratefu' debtor;
"But ance again, I dinna ken,
"We'll ablens happen better."

  Then, hoest man! wi little wark,
    He soon forgat his ire;
  The patriarch he coost the sark,
    An' up an' till't like fire!

Tune—*Maggy Lauder*.

He till't, an' she till't,
    An' a' to mak a lad again;
The auld bold carl
    When he wan on to nod again.
An' he dang, an' she flang,
    An' a' to mak a laddie o't;
But he bor'd, an' she roar'd,
    An' coudna mak a lassie o't.

HERE'S HIS HEALTH IN WATER.

Tune—*In Johnston's Scotch Songs*, Vol. v, p. 494.

Altho' my back be at the wa',
    An' tho' he be the fau'tor;
Altho' my back be at the wa',
    A'll drink his health in water.
O wae gae by his wanton sides,
    Sae brawly's he could flatter;
I for his sake am slighted sair,
    An' dries the kintra clatter;
But let them sae whate'er they like,
    Yet, here's his health in water.

He follow'd me, baith out an' in,
    Thro' a' the nooks o' Killie;

He follow'd me baith out an' in,
    Wi' a' stiff stan'in ——;
But when he gat between my legs,
    We made an unco spatter;
An' haith, I trow, I soupled it,
    Tho' bauldly he did blatter;
But tho' my back is at the wa',
    Yet here's his health in water.

I REDE YOU BEWARE O' THE RIPPLES.

Tune—*The Taylor's Faun Thro' the Bed, &c.*

I rede you beware o' the ripples, young man;
I rede you beware o' the ripples, young man;
Tho' the saddle be saft, ye needna ride aft,
For fear that the girdin' beguile you, young man.

I rede you beware o' the ripples, young man;
I rede you beware o' the ripples, young man;
Tho' music be pleasure, tak music in measure,
Or ye may want win' i' your whistle, young man.

I rede you beware o' the ripples, young man;
I rede you beware o' the ripples, young man;
Whate'er ye bestow, do less than ye dow,
The mair will be thought o' your kindness, young man.

I rede you beware o' the ripples, young man;
I rede you beware o' the ripples, young man;
Gif ye wad be strang, an' wish to live lang,
Dance less wi' your a-se to the kipples, young man.

ACT SEDURUNT O' THE COURT O' SESSION.

Tune—*O'er the Muir Amang the Heather.*

In Embrugh town they've made a law,
    In Embrugh at the court o' session;
That stan'in' —— are fau'tors a',
    An' guilty o' a high transgression.

    Decreet o' the court o' session,
    Act sedurunt o' the session;
    That stan'in' —— are fau'tors a',
    An' guilty o' a high transgression.

An' they've provided dungeons deep,
    Ilk lass has ane in her possession;
Until the fau'tors wail an' weep,
    They there shall lie for their transgression.

    Decreet o' the court o' session,
    Act sedurunt o' the session,
    The rogues in pouring tears shall weep,
    By act sedcrunt o' the session.

THE LASS O' LIVISTON.

The bonnie lass o' Liviston,
    Her name ye ken, her name ye ken;
An' ay the welcomer ye'll be,
    The farther ben, the farther ben.
An' she has written in her contract
    To lie her lane, to lie her lane;
An' I hae written in my contract,
    To claw her wame, to claw her wame.

The bonnie lass o' Liviston,
    She's berry brown, she's berry brown;
An' ye winna true her lovely locks,
    Gae farther down, gae farther down.
She has a black and a rolling eye,
    An' a dimplit chin, an' a dimplit chin;
An' no to prie her rosie lips,
    Wad be a sin, wad be a sin.

The bonnie lass o' Liviston,
    Cam in to me, cam in to me;
I wat wi' baith ends o' the busk,
    I made me free, I made me free.
I laid her feet to my bedstock,
    Her head to the wa', her head to the wa';
An' I gied her wee coat in her teeth,
    Her sark an' a', her sark an' a'.

SHE'S HOY'D ME OUT O' LAUDERDALE.

There liv'd a lady in Lauderdale,
  She lo'ed a fiddler fine;
She lo'ed him in her chamber,
  She lo'ed him in her mind;
She made his bed at her bed-stock,
  She said he was her brither;
But she's hoy'd him out o' Lauderdale,
  His fiddle an' a' thegither.

First when I came to Lauderdale,
  I had a fiddle guid,
My sounding pin stood like an aik
  That grows in the Lauder-wood;
But now my sounding pin's gaen down,
  An' tint the foot forever;
She's hoy'd me out o' Lauderdale,
  My fiddle an' a' thegither.

First when I came to Lauderdale,
  Your ladyship can declare,
I play'd a bow, a noble bow,
  As e'er was strung wi' hair;
But, downa do's come o'er me now,
  An' your ladyship winna consider;
She's hoy'd me out o' Lauderdale,
  My fiddle an' a' thegither.

YE HAE LIEN WRANG, LASSIE.

Tune—*Up an' Waur Them a', Willie.*

Ye hae lien wrang lassie,
    Ye've lien a' wrang;
Ye've lien in some unco bed,
    And wi' some unco man.

Your rosy cheeks are turned so wan,
    Ye're greener than the grass, lassie;
Your coatie's shorter by a span,
    Yet diel ae inch the less, lassie.

    Ye hae lien, &c.

Ye've loot the ponnie o'er the dyke,
    An' he's been i' the corn, lassie;
For ay the brose ye sup at e'en,
    Ye bock them or the morn, lassie.

    Ye hae lien, &c.

For lightly lap ye o'er the knowe,
    An' thro' the wood ye sang, lassie;
But herryin' o' the foggie byke,
    I fear ye've got a stang, lassie.

    Ye hae lien, &c.

WILL YE NA, CAN YE NA LET ME BE.

TUNE—*I Hae Laid a Herrin' in Saut.*

There liv'd a wife in Whistlecockpen,
    Will ye na, can ye na let me be;
She brews good jill for gentlemen,
    An' ay she waggit it wantonlie.

The night blew sair wi' wind an' weet,
    Will ye na, &c.
She shaw'd the traveler Ben to slee,
    An' ay, &c.

She saw a sight below his sark,
    Will ye na, &c.
She wadna wanted for a mark,
    An' ay, &c.

She saw a sight aboon his knee,
    Will ye na, &c.
She wadna wanted it for three,
    An' ay, &c.

O whare live ye, an' what's your trade?
    Will ye na, &c.
I am a thresher guid, he said,
    An' ay, &c.

An' that's my flail an' workin' graith,
　Will ye na, &c.
An' noble tools, quo' she, by my faith!
　An' ay, &c,

I wad gie a browst, the best I hae,
　Will ye na, &o.
For a guid darg o' graith like thae,
　An' ay, &c.

I wad sell the hair frae off my tail,
　Will ye na, &c.
To buy our Andrew, siccan a flail,
　An' ay, &c.

THE CASE OF CONSCIENCE.

Tune—*Auld Sir Symon, the King.*

I'll tell you a tale of a wife,
　An' she was a whig an' a saunt,
She liv'd a most sanctified life,
　But whyles she was fash'd wi' her ——.

Poor woman, she gaed to the priest,
　An' to him she made her complain;
There's naithing that troubles my breast,
　Sae sair, as the sins o' my ——.

He bade her to clear up her brow,
   An' no be discourag'd upon't,
For haly guid women enow,
   Are mony times waur'd wi' their ——.

It's nocht but Belzebub's art,
   An' that's the mair sign of a saunt;
He kens that ye're pure at the heart,
   So he levels his darts at your ——.

O you that are called an' free,
   Elekit an' chosen a saunt,
Wilt break the eternal degree,
   Whate'er ye do wi' your ——.

An' now, wi' a sanctified kiss,
   Let's kneel an' renew the cov'nant,
It's this — and it's this — and it's this —,
   That settles the pride o' your ——.

Devotion blew up to a flame,
   Nae words can do justice upon't;
The honest auld carlin gaed hame,
   Rejoicin' an' clawin' her ——.

COMIN' O'ER THE HILLS O' COUPAR.

Tune—*Ruffian's Rant.*

Comin' o'er the hills o' Coupar,
Comin' o'er the hills o' Coupar,
Donald in a sudden wrath,
He ran his highland dirk into her.

Donald Brodie met a lass
Comin' o'er the hills o' Coupar;
Donald, wi' his highland hand,
Graipit a' the bits about her.
   Comin' o'er, &c.

Weel I wat she was a quine,
 Wad made a body's mouth to water;
Our Mess John, we's auld gray pow,
 His haly lips wad licket at her.
   Comin' o'er, &c.

Up she started in a fright,
 An' thro' the braes what she could bicker;
Let her gang, quo' Donald now,
 For in him's nerse my shot is siker.
   Comin' o'er, &c.

BROSE AND BUTTER.

Jenny sits up i' the laft,
  Jockie wad fain be at her;
But there cam a wind out o' the west,
  Made all the winuocks to scatter.

  O gie my love brose, brose,
    O gie my love brose an' butter;
  For nane in Carrick wi' him,
    Can please a lassie better.

The lavrock lo'es the grass,
  The pairtrick lo'es the stibble;
An' hey for the gard'ner lad,
  To gully awa wi' his dibble!

    O gie, &c.

My daddie sent me to the hill,
  To pu' my Minnie some heather;
An' drive it in your fill,
  Ye're welcome to the leather.

    O gie, &c.

The mouse is a merry wee beast,
  The moudiewart wants the een;

An' o for a touch o' the thing,
   I had in my nieve yestreen.
       O gie, &c.

We a' were fou yestreen,
   The night shall be its brither;
An' hey for a merry pin,
   To nail twa wames togither.
       O gie, &c.

THE SIMMER MORN.

Tune—*Push About the Jorum.*

When maukin-bucks, at early ——,
   In dewy glens are seen, sir,
When birds, on boughs, tak aff their mows,
   Amang the leaves sae green, sir;
Latona's son looks liquorish on
   Dame Nature's grand impetus,
Till his Pego rise, then westward flies,
   To r——r Madam Thetis.

Yon wand'ring rill that marks the hill,
   An' glances o'er the brae, sir,
Sides by a bower, where mony a flower,
   Sheds fragrance on the day, sir;

There Damon lay, wi' Sylvia gay,
  To love they thought no crime, sir;
The wind birds sang, the echoes rang,
  While Damon's —— beat time, sir.

First, wi' the thrush, his thurst au' push,
  Had compass large an' long, sir;
The blackbird next, his tunefu' text,
  Was bolder, clear an' strong, sir;
The linnet's lay came then in play,
  An' the lark that soared aboon, sir;
Till Damon, firce, mistim'd his ——,
  An' —— quite out of time, sir.

SHE GRIPPET AT THE GIRTEST O'T.

Tune—*East Nook o' Fife.*

Our bride flate, and our bride flang,
But lang before the lav'rock sang,
She paid him twice for ev'ry bang,
  An' grippet at the girtest o't.

Our bride turn'd her to the wa',
But long before the cock did craw,
She took him by the —— au' a',
  An' grippet at the girtest o't,

WHA'LL KISS ME NOW.

Tune—*Comin' Thro' the Rye.*

O wha'll kiss me now, my Jo,
    An' wha'll kiss me now;
A soger wi' his bandiliers
    Has bang'd my belly fu'.

O I hae tint my rosy cheek,
    Likewise my waist sae sma';
O wae gae by the soger lown,
    The soger did it a'.
        An' wha'll, &c.

Now I maun thole the scornfu' sneer,
    O' mony a saucy quine;
When, curse upon her godly face!
    Her —— as merry's mine.
        An' wha'll, &c.

Our dame hauds up her wanton tail,
    As due as she gaes lie;
An' yet misca's a young thing,
    The trade if she but try.
        An' wha'll, &c.

Our dame can lae her ain gudeman,
    An' —— for glutton greed;

An' yet misca' a poor thing
That's —— for its bread.
  An' wha'll, &c.

Alake! sae sweet a tree as love,
Sic bitter fruit should bear!
Alake, that e'er a merry ——,
Should draw a sautty tear.
  An' wha'll, &c.

But deevil tak the lousy loun,
Denies the bairn he got!
Or lea's the merry —— he lo'ed,
To wear a ragged coat.
  An' wha'll, &c.

YESE GET A HOLE TO HIDE IT IN.

Tune—*Waukin' o' the Fauld.*

O will ye speak at our town,
  As ye come frae the fair?
An' yese get a hole to hide it in,
Yese get a hole to hide it in;
Will yese speak at our town,
  As ye come frae the fair?
Yese get a hole to hide it in,
  Will haud it a' an' mair.

O haud awa your hand, sir,
  Ye gar me ay think shame;
An' yese get a hole to hide it in,
Yese get, &c.
O haud away your hand, sir,
  Ye gar me ay think shame;
An' yese get a hole to hide it in,
  An' think yoursel at hame.

O will ye let abee, sir?
  Toots! now, ye've reft my sark,
An' yese get a hole to hide it in,
Yese get, &c.
O will ye let abee, sir,
  Toots! now, ye've reft my sark;
An' yese get a hole to hide it in,
  Whare ye may work your wark.

O haud awa your hand, sir
  Ye're like to pit me daft;
An' yese get a hole to hide it in,
An' yese get, &c.
O haud awa your hand, sir,
  Ye're like to pit me daft;
An' yese get a hole to hide it in,
  To keep it warm an' saft.

O haud it in your hand, sir,
   Till I get up my claes;
An' yese get a hole to hide it in,
Yese get, &c.
O haud it in your hand, sir,
   Till I get up my claes,
And yese get a hole to hide it in,
   To keep it frae the flaes.

DUNCAN MACLEERIE.

Tune—*Jocky Macgill.*

Duncan Macleerie an' Janet, his wife,
The gaed to Kilmarnock to buy a new knife;
But instead of a knife, they coft but a bleerie;
We're very weel serv'd, Janet, quo' Duncan Macleerie.

Duncan Macleerie has got a new fiddle,
It's a' strung wi' hair, an' a hole in the middle;
An' ay when he plays on't, his wife looks sae cheery,
Very weel done, Duncan, quo' Janet Macleerie.

Duncan, he play'd till his bow its grew greasy;
Janet grew fretfu', an' unco uneasy;
Hoot, quo' she, Duncan, ye're unco soon weary;
Play us a pibrobh, quo' Janet Macleerie.

Duncan Macleeric he play'd on the harp,
An' Janet Macleeric she danc'd in her sark;
Her sark it was short, her —— it was hairy,
Very weel danc'd, Janet, quo' Duncan Macleeric.

DUNCAN DAVIDSON.

There was a lass, they ca'd her Meg,
    An' she gae'd o'er the muir to spin;
She fied a lad to lift her leg,
    They ca'd him Duncan Davidson.
        Fal lal, &c.

Meg had a muff, an' it was rough,
    'Twas black without and red within;
An' Duncan, case he got the cauld,
    He slipt his Highland Pistol in.
        Fal lal, &c.

Meg had a muff, an' it was rough,
    An' Duncan strak twa neivfu' in;
She clasp'd her heels about his waist,
    I thank you, Duncan! yerk it in.
        Fal lal, &c.

Duncan made her hurdies dreep,
 In highland wrath, then Meg did say;
O gang he east, or gang he west,
 His —— will be no dry the day.
　　Fal lal, &c.

THEY TOOK ME TO THE HALY BAND.

Tune—*Clout the Cauldron.*

They took me to the haly band,
 For playing by my wife, sir;
An' lang an' sair they lectur'd me,
 For hadin' sic a life, sir.

I answer'd in na mony words,
 "What deil needs a' this clatter;
"As lang as she could keep the grip,
 "I aye was —— at her."

THE CHAMBERMAID.

Not far from town, a country squire,
 An open-hearted blade,
Had long confess'd a strong desire,
 To kiss the chambermaid,
 To kiss the chambermaid.

One summer's noon, quite fu' o' glee,
    He led her to the shade,
And all beneath the mulberry tree,
    He kiss'd the chambermaid.
    He kiss'd the chambermaid.

The parson's wife' from window high,
    The am'rous pair survey'd;
And softly wished, none can deny,
    She'd been the chambermaid;
When all was o'er, poor Betty cry'd
    Kind sir, I'm much afraid,
That woman there will tell your bride
    You kiss'd the chambermaid.

The squire conceiv'd a lucky-thought,
    That she might nor upbraid;
An' instantly the lady brought,
    Where he had kiss'd the maid;
Then all beneath the mulb'ry treet,
    Her ladyship was laid,
An' three times sweetly kiss'd was she,
    Just like her chambermaid.

Next morning came the parson's wife,
    (For scandal was her trade)
I saw your 'squire, ma'm, on my life,
    Great with your chambermaid;

When, cry'd the lady, where, and how?
   I'll soon discharge the jade;
Beneath the mulb'ry tree, I vow,
   He kiss'd your chambermaid.

This falsehood, cry'd her ladyship,
   Shall not my spouse degrade;
'Twas I chanc'd there to make a slip,
   And not my chambermaid:
Both parties parted in a pet,
   Not trusting what was said;
And Betty keeps her service yet,
   The pretty chambermaid.

DON'T BE IN SUCH A HURRY.

One winter's night, in am'rous mood,
   I went to see my Sally,
The rain beat hard, the wind blew loud,
   Which dreary made me dally;
'Twas late, and Sal had gone to bed,
   I knock'd her in a flurry,
Make haste, I cried; I'm here she said,
   Don't be in such a hurry.

Down stairs she came and let me in,
　All in her shift, I vow, sir,
And tho' I wet was to the skin,
　I felt I scarce know how, sir:
I kiss'd her lips, her bubbies prest,
　Which put me in a flurry,
With ligh'ning in her eyes, she cried,
　Don't be in such a hurry.

Up stairs we went, and into bed,
　When love soon crowned our wishes,
My vig'rous nature soon was spent,
　In such transporting blisses:
The morning came, I rose to part,
　When she cried, in a flurry,
When e'er you come this way again,
　Don't be in such a hurry.

SYLVIA.

As Sylvia on her arm reclining,
　In a shady cool retreat,
All in disabille, designing—fal lal, &c.
　To elude the sultry heat;
　　All in disabille, designing,
　　　To elude the sultry heat.

All reveal'd, she thought no stander-
By could view the lovely fair,
While cool zephyrs came and fann'd her—fal lal, &c.
Beauteous face with fragrant air.
  While cool, &c.

Thus the happy nymph lay panting,
Sighing for her absent swain,
All extended, she lay wanting—fal lal, &c.
Him to ease her lovesick pain.
  All extended, &c.

In the nick, the swain who won her,
Thro' the cool retreat drew near,
And with transport gaz'd upon her—fal lal, &c.
Charms repos'd in slumber there.
  And with transport, &c.

Love persuaded 'twas no sin, to
Vent his flame without delay,
So he boldly entered into—fal lal, &c.
Tales of love and am'rous play.
  So he boldly, &c.

His moving tale so wrought upon her,
That in pity to his pain,

She gave broad hints that he should once more—fal lal, &c.
Tell it o'er to her again.
    She gave, &c.

ANDREW AN' HIS CUTTIE GUN.

    Blythe, blythe, blythe was she,
      Blythe was she but an' ben;
    An' weel she looed it in her nieve,
      But better when it slippit in.
        Blythe, blythe, &c.

When a' the lave gaed to their bed,
    An' I sat up to clean the shoon,
O wha think ye cam jumpin' in,
    But Andrew an' his cuttie gun.
        Blythe, blythe, &c.

Or e'er I wist he laid me back,
    An' up my gammon to my chin;
An' ne'er a word to me spak,
    But littit out his cuttie gun.
        Blythe, blythe, &c.

The bawsent bitch she left the whalps,
An' hunted round us at the fun,
As Andrew fodgel'd wi' his doup,
An' fir'd at me the cuttie gun.
    Blythe, blythe, &c.

O some delights in cuttie stoup,
An' some delights in cuttie-mun,
But my delights, an a—elius coup,
Wi' Andrew an' his cuttie gun.

Blythe, blythe, blythe was she,
Blythe was she but an' ben;
An' weel she looed it in her nieve,
But better when it slippit in.

O GAT YE ME WI' NAETHING.

    Tune—*Jacky Latin.*

Gat ye me, O gat ye me,
    An' gat ye me wi' naething;
A rock, a reel, a spinning wheel,
    A gude black ——— was ae thing.

A tocher fine, o'er muckle faar,
    When sic a scullion gat it;
Indeed, o'er muckle far gudewife,
    For that was ay the fau't o't.

But had your tongue now, Luckie Lang,
  O had your tongue an' jander,
I held the gate till you I met,
  Syne I began to wander;
I tint my whistle an' my sang,
  I tint my peace and pleasure;
But your green grave now, Luckie Lang,
  Wad airt me to my treasure.

O CAN YE LABOUR LEE, YOUNG MAN.

Tune—*Sir Arch. Grant's Strathspey.*

O can ye labour lee, young man?
  O can ye labour lee!
Gae back the road ye cam again,
  Ye never shall scorn me.

I fee'd a man at Martinmas,
  Wi' arle pennies three;
But a' the faut I had to him,
  He coudna labour lee.

    An' can ye, &c.

A stibble rig is easy plough'd,
  An' fallow land is free;

> But what a silly coof is he,
> That canna labour lee.
>
> An' can ye, &c.
>
> The spretty bush, an' benty knowe,
> The ploughman points his sock in,
> He sheds the roughness, lays it bye,
> An' bauldly ploughs his yokin'.
>
> O can ye, &c.

OUR JOHN'S BRAK YESTREEN.

Tune—*Gramachree.*

> Twa neebor wives sat i' the sun,
> A twynin' at their rocks
> An' they an argument began,
> An' a' the plea was ——.
>
> 'Twas, wether they were sinners strang?
> Or wether they were bane?
> An' how they row'd about their thumb,
> An' how they stan't them lane?
>
> First, Rachie gae her rock a rug,
> An' Syne she claw'd her tail;
> "When our Tam draws on his breeks,
> "It waigles like a flail."

Says Bess, "ther're bane I will maintain,
"An' proof in hau' I'll gie;
"For our Jock's it brak yestreen,
"An' I fand it on my thie."

GIE THE LASS HER FAIRIN'.

Tune—*Cauld Kail in Aberdeen.*

O gie the lass her fairin', lad,
   O gie the lass her fairin',
An' something else she'll gie to you,
   That's waly' worth the wearin';
Syne coup her o'er amáng the creels,
   When ye hae taen your brandy,
The mair she bangs the less she squeals,
   An' hey for houghmagundie.

Then gie the lass her fairin', lad,
   O gie the lass her fairin',
An' she'll gie you a hairy thing,
   An' of it be na sparin';
But coup her o'er amang the creels,
   An' bar the door wi' baith your heels,
The mair she gets the less she squeals;
   An' hey for houghmagundie.

THE COOPER O' CUDDY.

TUNE—*Bab at the Bowster.*

We'll hide the cooper behind the door,
    Behind the door, behind the door,
We'll hide the cooper behind the door,
    For fear o' the gudeman, O.

The cooper o' cuddy cam here awa,
    He ca'd the girds out o' us a';
An' our gudewife has gotten a fa',
    That anger'd the silly gudeman, O.
        We'll hide, &c.

He sought them out, he sought them in,
    Wi' diel hae her, an' diel hae him;
But the bodie he was so doited an' blin',
    He wist na whare he was gaun, O.
        We'll hide, &c.

They cooper'd at e'en, they coopered at morn,
    Till our gudeman has gotten the scorn;
On ilka brow she's planted a horn,
    An' swears that there they shall stan', O.
        We'll hide, &c.

THERE CAM A CADGER.

Tune—*Claut the Cauldron.*

There cam a cadger out o' Fife,
    I wat na how they ca'd him;
He play'd a trick to our gudewife,
    Whan fient a body bad him.
        Fal lal, &c.

He took a lang thing, stout an' strang,
    An' strack it in her gavel;
An' ay she swore she fand the thing,
    Gae borin' by her navel.
        Fal lal, &c.

DEAR VARIETY.

Let the philosophic wise,
Preach up rules the gay despise;
Let the hoary bearded sage,
Censure follies of the age;
Yet while brisk the vital tide,
Pleasure, thou shalt be my guide;
Live, oh goddess! live with me,
All in dear variety.

Dwell thou, love, within my breast,
Just enough to make me blest;
Let thy sweet incessant spring,
But protect me from the sting!
Be the passion unconfin'd,
Under no restraint the mind;
But like birds, as fond and free,
Pleas'd with dear variety.

Keep, oh Plutus! all thy wealth,
Give me competence and health;
Care surrounds the miser's hoard,
Pain attends the spendthift's board;
Bacchus, in thy rosy bowl,
Let me sloke my thirsty soul;
But let reason wait on thee,
Reason prompts variety.

Life on wings of joy shall haste,
Gloomy thoughts the minutes waste;
We should banish care and fear,
Fate predestines all things here:
Hail to friendship, beauty, wine,
These make transient life divine!
May they ever live with me,
All in dear variety.

THE FEMALE PORCUPINE.

Tune—*Vaudeville to the Padlock.*

Puff'd up with pride, (that's sure to fall);
    A simple maid late made a pray'r
To mighty Jove, that at her call
    He'd condescend (with courteous care)
To make her haughty as his wife,
    And proudest of her sex to be,
For yet I have not in my life
    Seen one man good enough to me.

A strong-built youth, on self-same floor,
    O'erhearing what the damsel said,
Strait rose and op'd the chamber door,
    And thus addres'd the pretty maid,—
Thou form divine, I'm come from Jove,
    And you shall soon a peacock be;
O then, says she, sweet God of Love,
    Pray show me how the thing can be.

Quoth he, I must thus on your bed,
    Raise up your smock so white and clear;
What are you doing, sir? she said,
    But putting in a quill, my dear:
I'm filling up your tail, my love,
    And thus—, and thus—, I must begin,

To do the work of mighty Jove,
   I'm sticking the first feather in.

A while they lay with swimming eyes,
   Oft he repeated kisses keen,
With lifted looks and heaving sighs,
   She said,— what does such kisssng mean?
My sweet, says he, to make your bill—
   Pish! psha! says she, that won't prevail—
Give me again your juicy quill,
   And stock more feathers in my tail.

I own you've done your work complete,
   And Jove has granted me my will,
Your feathers are both strong and neat,
   But let each feather have a quill.
A quill each hour of that same size,
   An' stongly stuff'd in this same part,
Will make my plumes of feathers rise,
   And win my fortune and my heart.

He cries, Jove whispers me, my fair,
   Obey the lovely lady's will,
And in your work I will take care
   That ev'ry feather has a quill:
Says she, my dear, then ere we part,
   O stick them thick, I'll ne'er repine,

I'll bear the smart with all my heart,
Till I become a porcupine.

LANGOLEE.

Ye botanists yield, I've discovered a root,
  Adapted to females of ev'ry degree;
How sovereign its virtues, balsamic its fruit;
  I hope you'll believe when you hear it from me.
Langolee is the Irish name of it;
Great in this nation already the fame of it;
Make but one trial, and quickly you'll see,
There's nothing comparing to Langolee.

When winter's keen blasts are corrected by spring,
  The lads and lasses of every town,
Dance round at the Maypole, for Maypole's the thing,
  Expressive of Lango's high fame and renown.
Langolee, wonderful medicine,
Sensitive plant, and beggar's best bennison;
How happy the island productive of thee,
Thou root of all roots, thou Langolee.

Ye matrons afflicted with colic or wind,
  Hysterics, or what you may call it, from me,
Restorative Lango, a medicine you will find,
  'Twill enliven your spirits most wonderously.

Langolee, sweet is the juice of it;
Gently compress it, and gently make use of it.
In city or country, wherever it be,
The sweets are the same of my Langolee.

Ye girls of cities, with nervous disorders,
If from declinsions you'd wish to be free,
Ye dear little gentles pray take what I order,
The Hibernian colt's foot call'd Langolee.
Langolee, to prevent imposition,
You'll get it from none but the Irish physician;
Made up in triangular pills for admission:
The pectoral nostrum of Langolee.

DARBY'S KEY TO UNA'S LOCK.

'Twas in a sweet May morning,
When violets were springing, O!
The dew the meads adorning,
The larks melodious singing, O!
The rose-trees, by each breeze,
Were gently wafted up and down,
And the primrose, than then blows,
Bespangled nature's verdant gown.

The purling rill, the murm'ring stream,
  Stole gently thro' the lofty grove;
Such was the time, when Darby
  Stole out to meet his barefoot love.
      Tol, lol, &c.

Sweet Una was the tightest,
  Genteelest of the village dames;
Her eyes they were the brightest
  That e'er set youthful hearts in flames.
  Her lover, to move her,
    By every art, in vain essayed
  In ditty, for pity,
    This lovely maid he often pray'd;
But she, perverse, his suit denied.
Sly Darby, being enrag'd at this,
Resolv'd, when they next met, to seize
The lock that scatters Una's p–ss.
      Tol, lol, &c.

Beneath a lofty old oak
  She sat, with cow and milking pail;
From lily hands, at each stroke,
  In flowing streams the milk doth steal.
  With peeping and creeping,
    Sly Darby now comes on a pace,
  In raptures, the youth sees
    The blooming beauty of her face;

Fir'd with her charms, he now resolves
    No longer to delay his bliss,
But instantly to catch the lock
    That scatters pretty Una's p–ss.
        Tol, lol, &c.

Within his arms he seiz'd her,
    And press'd her to his panting breast;
What more could have appeas'd her,
    But oaths which Darby meant in jest:
    He swore he'd adore her,
        And to her ever constant prove;
    He'd wed her, he'd bed her,
        And none on eatrh but her he'd love.
With vows like these, he won her o'er,
    And hop'd she'd take it not amiss,
If he'd presume to catch the lock
    That scatters pretty Una's p–ss.
        Tol, lol, &c.

Upon her back he laid her,
    Turn'd up her smock, so lily white;
With joy the youth survey'd her,
    Then gaz'd with wonder and delight.
    Her thighs were as snow fair,
        And just between appear'd a crack;
    The lips red, and overspread
        With curling hairs of jetty black.

Transported, Darby now beholds
  The sum of all his promis'd bliss,
And instantly he catch'd the lock
  That scatters pretty Una's p-ss.
    Tol, lol, &c.

His —— stood erected,
  His breeches down about his heels;
And what he long expected,
  He now with boundless rapture feels.
    Now enter'd, concenter'd,
      The beauteous maid lay in a trance;
    His —— goes like elbows
      Of fiddlers in a country dance.
The melting Una, now she cries,
  I'd part with life for joy like this;
With show'rs of bliss they jointly oil'd
  The lock that scatters Una's p-ss.
    Tol, lol, &c.

LULLABY.

Nancy, on a sofa lying,
  Caught, by chance, my raptur'd eye,
'Twixt her lily thighs, I gently,
  Sighing, plac'd my lullaby.
    Lullaby, lullaby, lullaby, lullaby,
    Sighing, plac'd my lullaby.

Quickly waking to the motion,
　Thus the lovely maid did cry,
"Women's fears, they're all a notion,
"How I'm soothed with lullaby."
　　Lullaby, &c.

Seven times in transporting blisses,
　Each did with the other vie;
Still her hand fresh vigour courting,
　As'k again for lullaby.
　　Lullaby, &c.

Tell me, dearest youth, if heaven,
　Be like this, then let me die;
Every night repeat the seven,
　Kill me with your lullaby.
　　Lullaby, &c.

THE CRICKET AND CRAB-LOUSE.

Tune—*Derry, Down, Down.*

As a crab-louse and flea went ahunting together,
They took shade in a rose from the heat of the weather;
This rose being fairer by far than the rest,
Was pluck'd by a lady, and stuck in her breast.

These hunters, perceiving a fair open track,
'Twixt two hills white as snow, took the road to her back;
Then, descending all day, reach'd the valley by night,
Oh ho! says the flea, here's an inn, I'll alight.

And I, says the crab-louse, will pass through this gap,
And, without the expense of an inn, take my nap;
I see a small hovel, and at it I'll stay,
So onward he jogg'd, to go sleep in the hay.

Thus possess'd of the settlements, back and frontier,
They hop'd from encroachments to keep themselves clear;
But both climate and foe had combin'd to annoy,
Nor would grant them a day their domains to enjoy.

For scarce had the flea taken one sip at his claret,
When the tenement shook from the cellar to garret;
Then a strange rumbling noise thro' the passage did roar,
Which drove this poor tippler behind the street door.

A sultress salt shower succeeded this storm,
Which drove him, all drench'd, like a hare, from its form;
Thro' the smoking wet grass he was glad for to run,
And swore, while he liv'd, that damned inn he would shun.

In the morning he meets with the crab-louse, his friend,
Relates his adventure, and soon makes an end;

Now, with me, says the crab, still worse fortune took place;
When I tell you my sufferings you'll pity my case.

In the midst of my bay I discover'd a cave,
As deep as a coal-pit, as dark as a grave;
With black thorns, and brambles all growing about;
So I fear'd to go in, lest I should not get out.

Soon a giant approach'd me, a Cyclops, I ween,
For only one eye in his forehead was seen,
Who drove me from brier to bramble, full sore;
Then entering himself, thrust me in before.

Tho' wide was the cave, he could hardly get in,
So in forcing the passage, he rubb'd off the skin;
Then he strain'd and he swell'd, and still bigger he grew,
Till forth from his forehead his brains at me flew.

Now, the fray at an end, like a half-drowned mole,
I crept up to the top, to peep out of my hole;
And there I perceiv'd all at once, with surprise,
This giant was sunk to a pigmean size.

So I slily slipt by, overjoy'd to escape,
For I dreaded him still, tho' so alter'd in shape;

And here I am come in the pickel you see,
And the devil himself may go lodge there for me.

Tho', if I might advise it, these borders he'll shun,
Where he'll meet with a giant, as sure as a gun,
Who valuing nor blades, nor of bullets, a ——,
Like the Romans, attacks with a huge battering-ram.

For just as I passed him, I saw at his back,
Two large ponderous paving-stones tied in a sack;
Ay, ay, cried the flea, that same sack did I see,
For oft times with great vengeance he bang'd it at me.

But I manag'd so well, that I kept out of reach
Of this terrible engine that batters in breach;
And now that these perils are over our heads,
I hope that we may peaceably die in our beds.

SWEET SALLY.

My Sally is the blythest maid,
  Breath spicy, lips like rubies,
Youth in its wanton orbit plays,
  Snow hillocks are her bubbies:

Flush'd with the grape, the nymph I spied,
  My blood ran hurry scurry;
I breath'd my wishes; she replied,
  Don't be in such a hurry.

Her balmy breath I sweetly sipt,
  She vow'd she'd guard her honour,
Till, struggling, on the *carpet slipt*,
  And I, alas! upon her:
In such a case, what could I do?
  My senses in a flurry;
She cried as up her garments flew,
  Don't be in such a hurry.

She urg'd me on, and 'twixt her lips,
  My busy tongue kept plying,
In playful motion went her hips,
  Till breathless, fainting, dying:
In such a state entranced we lay,
  Our senses in a flurry,
I rose, she cried, nay, pray thee stay,
  Don't be in such a hurry.

Obeying, I again her prest,
  With sweet disorder panting;
And three times—you may guess the rest,
  I found no vigor wanting:

Drooping at last, she seiz'd *life's plant*,
   Swore she the charge would carry;
So soon, cried I—it rest doth want,
   Don't be in such a hurry.

Quite spent, no longer fit to strive,
   Says she, if your not able
To mount yourself, then let me drive,
   Your nag into the stable:
With that, she fierce began to ride
Like mad, all hurry skurry—
Quite spent at last, she faintly cried,
   Don't be in such a hurry.

THE DEEP NINE.

For London when with fav'ring gale,
   An Irish lad up channel steer'd,
Safe landed in the Chester mail,
   In London streets he soon appear'd;
The enamour'd fair ones round him clung,
And o'er his well-built shoulders hung,
   For his *deep nine.*

His *deep nine* gained him such renown,
   No rest had he by night or day,
By sounding half the girls in town,
   Two inches soon were worn away:

Yet still the fair ones round him clung,
And o'er his much shrunk shoulders hung,
For his *mark seven.*

At length, worn out with constant use,
Regardless they beheld the youth,
Who lately gave such matchless proofs
Of *length,* and *strength,* and *manly worth;*
No more the fair ones roung him clung,
His once fam'd *deep nine* lifeless hung,
Quarter less five.

THE LANG DOW.

Maggy lives at yon ha' head,
Andrew wons in yon'er glen;
Quoth Andrew to Maggie, will ye gae
An' cast your claes wi' mine—
Wi' my lang dow, my lang dow,
My lang tethery lang dow.

Na, na, quoth Maggie,
Siccan a thing maun never be,

Till ye gang to yon ha' house,
    An' speer my dad's guidwill o' me.
        Wi' your lang dow, &c.

Andrew's awa to yon ha' house,
    An' vows he tirles at the pin,
Wha's sae ready as wise Maggie
    To ask Andrew in—
        Wi his lang dow, &c.

Arms an' arms they meet thegither,
    Arms an' arms they laid them down,
Under Mag's doup lay Andrew's trouse,
    An' under her head lay her nain gown—
        Wi' his lang dow, &c.

The bridal day was fix'd upon,
    Mess John was sent to tie the knot;
The friends got a winsome feast,
    An' Mag an' Andrew lay down on the spot—
        Wi' his lang dow, &c.

Up gat the guidwife in a great fright,
    An' at her man gae many a pou,
I'll rin the hazard o' my life,
    That Mag and Andrew's yocket now—
        Wi' his lang dow, &c.

What's the matter? quoth the guidman,
   Mayna the lad kiss the lass?
First when I took thee by the han',
   Thou hadna a rag to cover thy a-se—
     But my lang dow, &c.

The neebours were a' assembled the neist day,
   An' axt her how she liket the dow?
She thank't them kindly for their pains,
   But said she kent it lang ere now—
     His lang dow, &c.

THE COURTSHIPS.

A beautiful lady, in fair London town,
Was woo'd by a Frenchman, a Teague, and a Clown
And others who would fain become bone of her bone,
Whose courtships I will relate one by one.
     With my fal de ral, &c.

The first who appear'd was a man of the mode,
A Frenchman by birth, Spittalfields his abode,
He address'd the fair creature with taste a-la-mode;
     And thus he said:—
Ah! mademoiselle, your eyes shinna like two burning
Glass in de sun, dat van peep from dem settas

My whole soul in a fire! begar you be de ver pret
Vench dat e'er I saw in my life—vi, if you would have
Me, I will just die immediatlee.

   With my fal de ral, &c.

The next who appear'd was a Yorkshire Clown,
To court this fair lady, he gallop'd the town;
He made her a long bow, and set himself down;
 And thus he said:—
Odds bodikins, I ne'er saw sic fair leady as you be,
Wite cheeks like ony churries, and then your bubbies
Are like ony good fat piece of beacon—if yause ha I
Ise ha you, and we'se make nea meare bians of the matter.

   With my fal de ral, &c.

The next was an Irishman, from Dublin come o'er,
And proud that he'd set foot on British shore;
Tho' cursedly proud, he was wretched poor;
 And thus he said:—
Arrah, my dear honey, had I you in dear Dublin
City, I'd sware you were the loveliest girl in all
London town, so I would, except my lord lieutenant's
Wife, and two or three thousand more of them;
And arrah, my dear honey, when you marry me, I'll make
You a present of a diamond ring, why, as big as ordinary
Murphy, fait, and so I will and I won't deceive you at all
At all, and by the holy poker of Dublin, and all the saints
Of her own country, I'll make you so happy a creature,

As no man alive, so I will; and every night I'll try
To plaze you with a little of my—

   Fal de ral, &c.

The next who appear'd was a swaggering blade,
Who, as we may say, was a soldier by trade,
He address'd this fair creature with words very big;
   And thus he said:—
Why, madam, you are as lovely as Venus, and I a
Strong built fellow, every way fitted to be your
Mars, as brave and as valliant as ever Cæsar and
Alexander were; but, blood and wounds, should I find a
Rival to your charms, I'd stake thousands; and to make
You happy, my love, every night I'd stake you—

   With my fal de ral, &c.

The next was a Quaker, so neat and so trim,
With a primitive face, and a very broad brim,
He address'd this fair lady, without moving a limb;
   And thus he said:—
Sarah, yea verily, thou art the maiden whom mine heart
Desirest, and thou hast found favor in my sight—
Ah! fair lump of clay, quit the ways of the vain,
And this thy Babylon, and untowards me as I
Look untowards thee! what comfort would one
Kiss give to the lip of the faithful! I pray thee

Consent that we may be one in the same flesh; then thou
Wilt be bone of my bone, and flesh of my flesh; and
Thou shalt grow as the vine tree, and spread forth thy
Roots as Lebanon;—now, Sarah, I will shuve thee; I'll
Not only shuve thee, but I'll ram-shuve thee;
I'll shuve thee as the ram shoveth the ewe, and
Make thy body fruitful; now, Sarah, I pray thee lift
Thy right leg, and then thy left leg, and let the prick
Of conscience enter thy virtuous body—

   With my fal de ral, &c.

 The last who appear'd was a jolly Jack Tar,
 Who, with Admiral Duncan, was enrich'd by the war,
 He thought with himself there was none on a par;
  And thus he said:—
Why, you must know, my little hearty, that I've been on
The lookout after you for sometime past—smite my crooked
Timbers if I han't, and am strongly inclined to capsize you
And take you in tow; for demme now, by the cut of your
Jib and breastwork, if you an't one of the tightest-rigg'd
Little frigates ever sailed; but to make no more palaver
About the matter, I am a tight young fellow, fit to overhau˙
All your tacling, who can hand, reef or put the two ends of
A rope together, with any man alive, so I can, and demme
My dear, if you can be better moor'd; suppose now, for
Instance, you were gunnel-deep in a good feather bed, and I

Alongside of you, mark you that, I would immediately give
Signal for chase, throw my grappling irons aboard,
Lash my main-yard to your larboard quarter; and if
I could not find your gang-way, then dem poor Jack,
   And his fal de ral, &c.

MY THING IS MY OWN.

I, a tender young maid, have been courted by many,
Of all sorts of trades as ever was any;
A spruce haberdasher first spake me fair,
But I should have nothing to do with small ware.
 My thing is my own, and I'll keep it so still,
 Yet other young lasses may do what they will.

A sweet-scented courtier did give me a kiss,
And he promis'd me mountains if I would be his;
But I'll not believe him, for it is too true,
Some courtiers do promise much more than they do.
   My thing is my own, &c.

A fine man of law did come out of the Strand,
To plead his own cause, with his *fee* in his hand;
He made a brave motion, but that would not do,
For I did dismiss him, and non-suit him too.
   My thing is my own, &c.

Next came a young fellow, a notable spark,
(With green bag and ink-horn, a justice's clerk,)
He pull'd out his warrant, to make all appear,
But I sent him away with a flea in his ear.
  My thing is my own, &c.

A master of music came with an intent,
To give me a lesson on my instrument;
I thank'd him for nothing, and bid him begone,
For my little fiddle should not be played on.
  My thing is my own, &c.

An usurer came, with abundance of cash,
But I had no mind to come under his lash;
He proffer'd me jewels and great store of gold,
But I wouldn'd mortgage my little freehold.
  My thing is my own, &c.

A blunt lieutenant next surprised my packet,
And fiercly began to riflle and sack it;
I muster'd my spirits up, and became bold,
And forc'd my lieutenant to guide his strong hold.
  My thing is my own, &c.

A crafty young bumpkin that was very rich,
And us'd with his bargains to go thro' each stitch,
Did tender a sum, but it would not avail,
That I should admit him my tenant *in tail*.
  My thing is my own, &c.

A fine dapper Taylor, with yard in his hand,
Did proffer his service to me at command;
He talked of a slit I had above the knee,
But I'll have no taylors to stitch it for me.
  My thing is my own, &c.

A gentlemen that did talk much of his grounds,
His horses, his setting-dogs, and his greyhounds,
Put in for a course, and us'd all his art;
But he miss'd of the sport—for puss would not start.
  My thing is my own, &c.

A pretty young squire new come to the town,
To empty his pockets, and so to go down,
Did proffer a kindness, but I would have none,
The same that he us'd to his mother's maid, Joan.
  My thing is my own, &c.

Now here I could reckon a hundred or more,
Besides all the gamesters recited before;
That made their addresses in hopes of a snap,
But young as I was, I understood trap.
  My thing is my own, and I'll keep it so still,
  Until I be married, say men what they will.

F

THE FAIR PENITENT.

A lovely lass to a friar came,
    To confess in the morning early;
In what art thou, my dear, to blame?
    Come, own it all sincerely.
I've done, sir, what I dare not name,
    With a lad that loves me dearly.

The greatest fault in myself I know,
    Is what I now discover:
Then you to Rome for that must go,
    Their discipline to suffer.
Lack-a-day, sir, if it must be so,
    Pray with me send my lover.

No, no, my dear, you do but dream,
    We'll have no double dealing;
But if with me you'll repeat the same,
    I'll pardon your past failing.
I must own, sir, though I blush for shame,
That your penance is prevailing.

FANNY.

When Fanny, blooming fair,
   First caught my ravish'd sight;
Struck with her shape and air,
   I felt a strange delight;
Whilst eagerly I gaz'd,
   Admiring every part,
And every female prais'd,
   She stole into my heart.

In her bewitching eyes,
   Ten thousand loves appear;
There Cupid basking lies,
   His shafts are boarded there;
Her blooming cheeks are dyed,
   With colour all their own,
Excelling far the pride,
   Of roses newly blown.

Her well-turn'd limbs confess,
   The lucky hand of love;
Her features all express,
   The beauteous Queen of Love.
What flames my nerves invade,
   When I behold the breast,
Of that too charming maid,
   Rise, suing to be press'd.

Venus round Fanny's waist,
　Has her own cestus bound,
With guardian Cupid's grac'd,
　Who dance the circle round.
How happy must he be,
　Who shall her zone unloose;
That bliss to all but me,
　May heaven and she refuse.

CHLOE.

Whenever, Chloe, I begin,
　Your heart, like mine, to move,
You tell me of the crying sin,
　Of unchaste, lawless love.

How can that passion be a sin,
　Which gave to Chloe birth?
How can those joys but be divine,
　Which makes a heaven on earth?

To wed, mankind the priests repann'd,
　By some sly fallacy,
And disobey'd God's great command:
　"Increase and multiply."

You say that love's a crime—content;
    Yet this allow you must,
More joy's in heaven if one repent,
    Than over ninety just.

Since then, dear girl, for heaven's sake,
    Repent, and be forgiv'n;
Bless me, and my repentance make
    A holy-day in heav'n.

KISSING.

Ye delicate lovelies, with leave I maintain,
    That happiness here you may find;
To yourselves I appeal for felicity's reign,
    When you meet with a man to your mind.

When gratitude friendship to softness unites,
    Inexpressive endearments arise;
Then hopes, fears, and fancies, strange doubts, and delights,
    Are announc'd by those tell tales, the eyes.

Those technical terms in the science of love,
    Cold schoolmen attempt to describe,

But how should they paint what they never can prove;
For tenderness knows not their tribe.

Of all the abuse on enjoyment that's thrown,
  The treatment love takes most amiss,
Is the rant of the coxcomb, the sot and the clown,
  Who pretend to indulge on a kiss.

The love of a fribble at self only aims:—
  For sots and clowns—class them with beasts;
No fibre, no atom, have they in their frames,
  To relish such delicate feasts.

In circling embraces, when lips to lips move,
  Description, O! teach me to praise,
The overture kiss to the op'ra of love—
  But beauty would laugh at the phrase.

Love's preludes are kisses, and, after the play,
  They fill up the pause of delight;
The rich repititions which never decay,
  The lips' silent language at night.

The raptures of kissing we only can taste,
  When sympathies equal inspire;
And while to enjoyment unbounded we haste,
  Their breath blows the coals of desire.

Again, and again, and again beauty sips;
  What feelings these pressures excite!
When fleeting life's stopp'd by a kiss of the lips,
  Then sinks in a sigh of delight.

LET HIM, FOND OF FIBBING.

Let him, fond of fibbing, invoke what he'll chuse,
Mars, Bacchus, Apollo, or Madam the Muse:
Great names in classical kingdom of letters;
But poets are apt to make free with their betters.

I scorn to say aught, save the thing that is true,
No beauties I'll plunder, yet give mine her due;
She has charms upon charms, such as few people may view,
She has charms—for the toothache, and eke for the ague.

Her lips—she has two, and her teeth they are white,
And what she puts into her mouth she can bite;
Black and all black her eyes; but's what worth remark,
They are shut when she sleeps, and she's blind in the dark.

Her ears from her cheeks equal distance are bearing,
'Cause each side her head should go partners in hearing;
The fall of her neck's the downfall of beholders,
Love tumbles them in by the head and the shoulders.

Her waist is so-so, so waste no words about it;
Her heart is within it, her stays are without it;
Her breasts are so pair'd—two such breasts when you see,
You'll swear that no woman, yet born, e'er had three.

Her voice neither nightingales, no, nor canaries,
Nor all the wing'd warblers' wild whistling vagaries;
Nor shall I to instrument music compare it,
'Tis likely, if you was not deaf, you might hear it.

Her legs are proportion'd to bear what they've carried,
And equally pair'd as if happily married;
But wedlock will sometimes the best friends divide,
By her spouse so she's served, when he throws them aside.

Not too tall, nor too short, but I'll venture to say,
She's a very good size,—in the middling way;
She's—aye, that she is,—she is all—but I'm wrong,
Her *all* I can't say, for I've sung all my song.

THE UNION OF BEAUTY AND WINE.

One day at her toilet, as Venus began
    To prepare for her face-making duty,
Bacchus stood at her elbow, and swore that her plan
    Would not help it, but hinder her beauty.

A bottle young Semele held up to view,
    And begg'd she'd observe his directions—
This Burgundy, dear Cytherea, will do,
    'Tis a rogue that refines all complexions.

Too polite to refuse him, the bumper she sips,
    On his knees, the buck begg'd she'd encore;
The joy-giving goddess, with wine-moistened lips,
    Declar'd she would hob-nob once more.

Out of window each wash, paste and powder she hurl'd,
    And the god of the grape vow'd to join;
Shook hands, sign'd and seal'd, then bid fame tell the world,
    The union of beauty and wine.

CHASTITY.

Tune—*Good People, I'll Tell You no Rodomontade.*

I wonder, wuoth dame, as her spouse she embraces,
How strumpets can look, how they dare show their faces?
And those wicked wives, who from husbands' arms fly,
Lord! where do they think they must gō when they die?

But next day, by husband, with 'prentice boy caught,
When she from the bed was to toilet-glass brought,
Her head he held up, with his gentle rebuke—
My dear! you was wishing to know how whores look!

Turn your eyes to that table, at once you will see
What faces jades wear; then, my dear, behold me;
Your features confess the adulteress clear,
My visage exhibits how cuckolds appear.

You ask'd, where bad wives go! why really, my chick,
You must, with the rest of them, go to old nick;
If Belzebub don't such damn'd tenants disown,
For bad wives, he knows, make a hell of their own.

All the world would wed, if the clergy could show,
Any rule in the service to change i for o;
How happy the union of marriage would prove,
Not long as we liv'd join'd, but long as we love!

At his feet she sunk down, sorrow lent her such moans,
The resentment was gagg'd by her tears and her tones;
What could Hubby do then? what could then Hubby do?
But sympathy struck, as she cry'd, he cry'd too.

Oh! Corregoi! could I Sigisimunda design,
Or exhibit a Magdalen, Guido, like thine,
I would paint the fond look which the penitent stole,
That pierce'd her soft pardner, and sunk to his soul.

Transported to doating! he raised the distress'd,
And tenderly held her long time to his breast!
On the bed gently laid her, by her gently laid,
And the breach there was clos'd the same way it was made.

FOR A' THAT, AN' A' THAT.

The boniest lass that ye meet niest,
  Gie her a kiss, an' a' that,
In spite of ilka parish priest,
  Repenting stool, an' a' that,
    For a' that, an' a' that,
      Their mim-mou'd sangs, an' a, that,
    In time and place convenient,
      They'll do't themselves, for a' that.

Your patriachs, in days of yore,
  Had their handmaids, an' a' that;
O' bastard getts, some had a score,
  An' some had mair than a' that.
    For a' that, an' a' that,
      Your langsyne saunts, an' a' that,
    Were fonder o' a bonny lass,
      Than you or I, for a' that.

King Davie, when he waxed auld,
  An' bluid ran thin, an' a' that,
An' fand his c——s were growin' cauld,
  Could not refrain, for a' that.
    For a' that, an' a' that,
      To keep him warm, an' a' that,
    The daughters o' Jerusalem,
      Were wil'd for him, an' a' that.

Wha wadna pity thae sweet dames,
　Ile fumbled at, an' a' that,
An' rais'd their bluid up into flames,
　He coudna drown, an' a' that.
　　　For a' that, an' a' that;
　　　　He wanted *pith*, an' a' that;
　　　For, as to what we shall not name,
　　　　What could he do—but claw that.

King Solomon, prince o' divines,
　Wha proverks made, an' a' that,
Baith mistresses and concubines,
　In hundreds had, for a' that.
　　　For a' that, an' a' that,
　　　　Tho' preacher wise, an' a' that,
　　　The smuttiest sang that e'er was sung,
　　　　His *sang o' sangs* is a' that.

Then still I swear, a clever chiel
　Should kiss a lass, an' a' that,
Tho' priests consign him to the diel,
　As reprobate, an' a' that.
　　　For a' that, an' a' that,
　　　　Their canting stuff, an' a' that,
　　　They ken no mair wha's reprobate,
　　　　Than you or I, for a' that.

KEY-HOLE.

John Thomson keekit in at the key-hole,
   An' he keekit wi' the tail o' his e'e;
He saw the minister m————g the fiddler's wife,
   An' a guid lang bow drew he.

   An' ahee, an' ahee, an' ahee, quo' he,
   If this is nae the very vagabond,
   The self-same reverend vagabond,
   That on the stool set me.

BARM.

I'll trip upon trenchers, I'll dance upon dishes—
   My mither sent me for barm, for barm;
And thro' the kirk-yard I met wi' the laird,
   The silly puir body could do me nae harm.

But down i' the park, I met wi' the clark,
   And he gaed me my barm, my barm.

   *   *   *   *   *

LET ME IN THIS AE NIGHT.

O, lassie art thou sleeping yet;
Or are you waking I wad wit:
For love has bound me hand and fit,
    And I would fain be in, Jo.
O let me in this ae night, this ae, ae, ae night,
O let me in this ae night, and I'll ne'er come back agin, Jo.

The morn is in the term-day,
I maun away, I canna stay;
O pity me before I gae,
    And rise and let me in, Jo.

    O let me in, &c.

The night it is baith cauld and weet,
The morn it will be snaw and sleet;
My shoon are frozen to my feet,
    Wi' standing on the plain, Jo.

    O let me in, &c.

I am the laird o' windy-wa's,
I come na here without a cause,
And I hae gotten many fa's,
    Upon a naked wame, Jo.

    O let me in, &c.

My father's wauking on the street,
My mither she chamber keys does keep;
My chamber door does chirp and cheep,
And I darena let you in, Jo.
O gae your ways this ae night, this ae, ae, ae night,
O gae your ways this ae night, for I darena let you in, Jo.

But I'll come stealing saftly in,
And cannily mak little din;
And then the gate to you I'll find,
If you'll but direct me in, Jo.
    O let me in, &c.

Cast aff the shoon frae aff your feet,
Cast back the door up to the weet,
Syne into my bed you may creep,
And do the thing you ken, Jo.
O weel's me on this ae night, this ae, ae, ae night,
O weel's me on this ae night, that e'er I let you in, Jo.

She let me in sae cannily,
She let me in so privily,
She let me in sae cannily,
    To do the thing you ken, Jo.
    O weel's me, &c.

But e'er a' was done, and a' was said,
Out fell the bottom of the bed,
The lassie lost her maidenhead,
And her mither heard the din, Jo.
O the devil take this ae night, this ae, ae, ae night,
O the devil take this ae night, that e'er I let you in, Jo.

VENUS AND LOVE.

Ye sons of Anacreon, assist me to sing,
Of the fountain of Venus, the rivulet spring,
'Tis a mystical mirror, tho' hidden from sight,
Can attarct even age to the fount of delight;
For the soul lost in transport is wafted above,
When you dip in the fountain of Venus and Love.

  For the soul, &c.

It dwells in a valley by moss circled round,
And tho' ever plum'd no bottom e'er found;
And here the wild spendthrift is welcome to range,
If he draws a-receipt by mutual exchange;
'Tis a spring of such sweets e'en stoics approve,
When they dip in the fountain of Venus and Love.

  'Tis a spring, &c.

The bank of this fountain's a beautiful red,
Its verge is inviting, tho' dang'rous to tread;

For oft in convulsions it ebbs and it flows,
And never so pleas'd as when't tells what it knows;
'Tis fierce in the conflict, yet meek as a dove,
If conquer'd, the fountain of Venus and Love,

  'Tis fierce, &c.

The richest of nectar this fountain distils,
That lies at the foot of the fairest of hills;
And the blossom that's lost in combating the suit,
Is often repaid with the choicest of fruit;
But vain is the task which thousands have strove,
To conquer the fountain of Venus and Love.

  But vain, &c.

THE TREE OF LIFE.

Come prick up your ears, and attend, sirs, awhile,
I'll sing ye a song that shall make ye to smile;
'Tis a faithful description of the tree of life,
So pleasing to every maid, widow and wife!

  Tol de rol, &c.

This tree is a cucculent plant, I declare,
Consisting only of one straight stem, I swear;
Its top sometimes looks like a cherry in May;
At other times more like a filbert, they say.

  Tol de rol, &c.

This tree universal, most countries produce;
But till eighteen years' growth 'tis not much fit for use;
Then nine or ten inches—for it seldom grows higher,
And that's sure as much as the heart can desire.
    Tol de rol, &c.

But chiefly in Ireland this plant it best thrives,
As well can be proved by their widows and wives;
Its root is so stout and long, I insist on't,
That most of their natives entirely subsist on't.
    Tol de rol, &c.

Some late virtuosi, this tree to improove,
Have cut off its fruit, call'd the Apples of Love;
But it never seeds after, nor is worth a louse,
Unless to make whistles for th' opera house.
    Tol de rol, &c.

Its juice taken inward's a cure for the spleen,
And removes in an instant the sickness call'd green;
Tho' sometimes it causes large tumours below,
Which disperse of themselves in nine months or so.
    Tol de rol, &c.

It cures all dissensions 'twixt husband and wife,
And makes her look pleasant thro' each stage of life;

By a right application it never can fail,
But then it must always be given in *tail*.

  Tol de rol, &c.

Ye ladies who long for a sight of this tree,
Take this invitation—come hither to me;
I have it just in the height of perfection,
Adapted for handling, and for injection.

  Tol de rol, &c.

THE MARRIAGE MORN.

The marriage morn I can't forget,
 My senses teem'd with new delight;
"Time," cry'd I, "haste the coming night,
"And, Hymen, give me sweet Lisette!"
 I whispered softly in her ear,
 And said, "the God of Night draws near."
O how she look'd! O how she smil'd! O how she sigh'd!
 She sigh'd—then spent a joyful tear.

Now nuptial night her curtain drew,
 And cupid's mandate was, "comence,
"With ardour break the virgin's fence!"
Then to the bed sweet Lisette flew—

'Twas heaven to view her as she lay,
And hear her cry, "come to me, pray!
O how I feel! O how I pant! O I shall die!
Shall die before the break of day."

Soon manhood rose with furious gust,
And Mars, when he lewd Venus view'd,
Ne'er felt his power so closely screw'd
Up to the standing-post of lust!
But when the stranger to her sight,
Sweet Lisette saw, in rampant plight!
O how she scream'd! O how she scream'd! O how she scream'd!
She scream'd—then grasp'd the dear delight.

Now lustful nature eager grew,
And longer could not wanton toy,
So rushing up the path of joy,
Quick from the fount love's liqour flew.—
At morn she cry'd, "full three times three,
"The vivid stream I felt from thee!
O how I'm eas'd! O how I'm pleas'd! gods, how I'm charm'd!
"I'm charm'd with rapt'rous three times three!"

THE END.

Papilio the rich, in the hurry of love,
Resolving to wed, to fair Arabel drove;
He made his proposals, he begg'd she would fix,—
What maid could say no to a new coach and six.

We'll suppose they were wed, the guests bid, supper done,
The fond pair in bed, and the stocking was thrown;
The bride lay expecting to what this would tend,
Since created a wife, wish'd to know for what end.

On the downy peach oft, as the gaudy fly rests,
The bridegroom's lips stopp'd, on love's pillows, her breasts;
All amazement, impassive, the heart-heaving fair,
With a sigh seem'd to prompt him, don't stay too long there.

Round her waist, and round such a waist circling his arms,
He raptures rehears'd on her unpossess'd charms;
Says the fair one, and gap'd, I hear all you pretend,
But now, for I'm sleepy, pray come to an end.

My love le'er shall end, Squire Shadow replied,
But still, unattempting, lay stretched at her side;
She made feints, as if something she meant to defend,
But found out, at last, it was all to no end.

In disdain, starting up from the impotent boy,
She, sighing, pronounc'd, there's an end of my joy;
Then resolv'd this advice to her sex she would send,
Ne'er to wed till they're sure they can wed to some end.

And what end is this? why the end which prevails,
Plough, ships, birds, fishes, are steer'd by their tails;
And tho' man and wife for the head may contend,
I'm sure they're best pleas'd when they gain t'other end.

The end of our wishes, the end of our wives,
The end of our loves, and the end of our lives,
The end of conjunction, 'twixt mistress and maid,
Tho' the head may design, has its end in the tail.

'Tis time tho' to finish, if aught I intend,
Lest, like a bad husband, I come to an end;
The ending I mean is, what none will think wrong,
And that is, to make now an end of my song.

SOFTLY.

Disguis'd, last night, I rush'd from home,
   To seek the place of my soul;
I reach'd by silent steps the dome,
   And to her chamber *softly* stole.

On a gay various couch reclin'd,
   In sweet repose I saw the maid;
My breast, like aspins to the wind,
   To love's alarums *softly* play'd.

Two fingers, then, to half expanse,
   I trembling op'd, with fear oppress'd,
With these I pull'd her veil askanse,
   Then *softly* drew her to my breast.

"Who art thou, wretch!" my angel cry'd;
   Whispering, I said,—"Thy slave, thy swain!
"But hush, my love, forbear to chide;
   Speak *softly*, lest some hear the strain."

Trembling with love, with hope, and fear,
   At length her ruby lips I press'd;
Sweet kisses oft,—mellifluous—dear—
   Softly I snatched—was *softly* bless'd.

"O let me," now inflam'd, I said,
"My idol clasp within these arms;
Remove the light," deep sigh'd the maid—
"Come *softly*, come—prevent alarms."

Now by her side with bliss I glow'd,
Swift flew the night in am'rous play;
At length the morning's herald crow'd,
When *softly* thence I bent my way.

SHE ROSE AND LOOT ME IN.

The night her silent sable wore,
And gloomy were the skies;
Of glitt'ring stars appear'd no more
Than those of Nelly's eyes.
When at her father's gate I knock'd,
Where I had often been,
She, shrouded only in her smock,
Arose and loot me in.

Fast lock'd within my close embrace,
She trembling stood asham'd;
Her swelling breast, and glowing face,
At ev'ry touch inflam'd.
My eager passion I obey'd,
Resolv'd the fort to win,
And her fond heart was soon betray'd,
To yield and let me in.

Then, then, beyond expressing,
    Transporting was the joy!
I knew no greater blessing,
    So blest a man was I.
And she, all ravish'd with delight,
    Bid me oft come again;
And kindly vow'd, that every night,
    She rise and let me in.

But ah! at last she proved wi' bairn,
    And sighing sat and dull,
And I, who was as much concern'd,
    Look'd e'en just like a fool.
Her lovely eyes with tears ran o'er,
    Repeating her rash sin;
She sigh'd and curs'd the fatal hour,
    That e'er she loot me in.

But who could cruelly deceive,
    Or from such beauty part?
I lov'd her so, I could not leave
    The charmer of my heart;
But wedd'd, and conceal'd our crime,
    Thus all was well again,
And now she thanks the happy time,
    That e'er she loot me in.

THE TAYLOR.

The tailor came to clout the claise,
    Sic a braw fellow,
He fill'd the house a' fou o' fleas,
    Daffin down, and daffin down;
He fill'd the house a' fou o' fleas,
    Daffin down and dilly.

The lassie slipt ayont the fire,
    Sic a braw hissey!
Oh! she was a' his heart's desire,
    Daffin down, daffin down;
Oh! she was a' his heart's desire,
    Daffin down and dilly

The lassie she fell fast asleep,
    Sic a braw hissey!
The tailor close to her did creep,
    Daffin down and daffin down;
The tailor close to her did creep.
    Daffin down and dilly.

The lassie waken'd in a fright,
    Sic a braw hissey!
Her maidenhead had ta'en the flight,
    Daffin down, and daffin down;

Her maidenhead had ta'en the flight,
Daffin down and dilly.

She sought it butt, she sought it ben,
　Sic a braw hissey;
And ln beneath the clocken-hen,
　Daffin down, and daffin down;
And in beneath the clocken-hen,
　Daffin down and dilly.

She sought it in the owsen-staw,
　Sic a braw hissey!
No, faith, quo she, it's quite awa',
　Daffin down, and daffin down;
No, faith, quo she, it's quite awa',
　Daffin down and dilly.

She sought it 'yont the knocking stane,
　Sic a braw hissy!
Some day, quo' she, 'twill gang its lane,
　Daffin down, and daffin down;
Some day, quo' she, 'twill gang its lane,
　Daffin down and dilly.

She ca'd the taylor to the court,
　Sic a braw hissey!

And a' the young men round about,
  Daffin down, and daffin down;
And a' the young men round about,
  Daffin down and dilly.

She gart the taylor pay a fine,
  Sic a braw hissey!
Gie me my maidenhead again,
  Daffin down, and daffin down;
Gie me my maidenhead again,
  Daffin down and dilly.

O what way wad ye ha't again?
  Sic a braw hissey!
Oh! just the way that it was ta'en,
  Daffin down, and daffin down;
Oh! just the way that it was ta'en,
  Daffin down and dilly.

THE MAID GOES TO THE MILL.

The maid's gane to the mill by night,
  Hech hey, sae wanton;
The maid's gane to the mill by night,
  Hey sae wanton she;

She's sworn by moon and stars sae bright,
That she should hae her corn ground,
That she should hae her corn ground,
   Mill and multure free.

Out then came the miller's man,
   Hech hey; sae wanton;
Out then came the miller's man,
   Hey sae wanton he;
He sware he'd do the best he can,
For to get her corn ground,
For to get, &c.
   Mill and multure free.

He put his hand about her neck,
   Hech hey, sae wanton;
He put his hand about her neck,
   Hey sae wanton he;
He dang her down upon a sack,
And there she got her corn ground,
And there she got, &c.
   Mill and multure free.

When other maids gaed out to play,
   Hech hey, sae wanton;
When other maids gaed out to play,
   Hey sae wantonlie;

She sigh'd and sobb'd, and wadna stay,
Because she got her corn ground,
Because she got, &c.
   Mill and multure free.

When forty weeks were past and gane,
   Hech hey, sae wanton;
When forty weeks were past and gane,
   Hey sae wantonlie;
The maiden had a braw lad-bairn,
Because she got her corn ground,
Because she got, &c.
   Mill and multure free.

Her mither bade her cast it out,
   Hech hey, sae wanton;
Her mither bade her cast it out,
   Hey sae wantonlie;
It was the miller's dusty clout,
For getting of her corn ground,
For getting, &c.
   Mill and multure free.

Her father bade her keep it in,
   Hech hey, sae wanton;
Her father bade her keep it in,
   Hey sae wantonlie;

It was the chief o' a' her kin,
Because she'd got her corn ground,
Because she'd got, &c.
  Mill and multure free.

THE WARMING PAN.

The coach arriv'd, impatient all,
For diff'rent things begin to call;
  But I, who have no trade
But love, for sweeter morsels try;
I search, and fix an am'rous eye,
  Upon the chambermaid.

I wait, and catch her as she flies,
From room to room with eager eyes;
  "My dear, permit my aid?"
I seize her, and she cries—a-done;
I kiss her quick, and let her run;
  The pretty chambermaid.

The supper comes, and Betty Grove,
'Tis Hebe waiting upon Jove;
  The reck'ning next is paid;

Yawning, the passengers retire,
I, burning like the kitchen fire,
  For Betty chambermaid.

Kneeling, my bed the beauty warms,
When, furious, I attack her charms:
  "Get out, you naughty man!"
The port is gained by quick surprise,
I kiss, she kicks, and faintly cries,
  "O! move the warming pan!"

There—there—, again—the bed—it burns,
I move—she moves—we move by turns,
  "What are you at, dear man?"
Hush! there's a noise—the bed, the joy,
Hark! hark! how sweet, my am'rous boy,
  Hold there—the warming pan.

Whene'er I pass the high north-road,
I knock at Betty's soft abode,
  Where happy I am laid;
The neatest inn, the softest thatch,
And tell me where a place can match,
  My pretty chambermaid.

ROGER AND MOLLY.

Beneath a weeping willow's shade,
Melting with love, fair Molly laid,
  Her cows were feeding by;
By turns she knit, by turns she sung,
While ever flow'd from Molly's tongue,
  "How deep in love am I!"

Young Roger chanc'd to stroll along,
And hearing Molly's am'rous song,
  And now and then a sigh;
Straight o'er the hedge he made his way,
And join'd with Molly in her lay;
  "How deep in love am I!"

The quick surprise made Molly blush,
"How rude," she cry'd, "now pray be hush!"
  Yet show'd a yielding eye;
"My needle's bent, my worsted's broke,
"Roger, I only meant in joke,
  "How deep in love am I!"

"You're rude—get out—I won't be kiss'd;
"Pray don't—yes do—be gone—persist!
  "Roger, I vow I'll cry!

"What are you at—you roguish swain?"
He answer'd in a dying strain,
"How deep in love am I!"

LYDY CHURNING.

Brim-full of love fat Lydy sat,
    Cheeks like a blooming plum;
Sweating, with all a maiden's strength,
    To make the butter come.

In vain she churn'd, in vain she try'd;
    O, would our Roger come!
For nothing but a Roger's strength,
    Can make my butter come.

Within the pantry Roger skulk'd,
    And heard this am'rous hum;
Then fixing fast on Lydy's churn,
    He made her butter come.

Lydy cried out,—Ro—oger—on—
That day may I be dumb,
If once I to—when you soon,
Can make my butter come.

THE BUMPER.

I can't for my life guess the cause of this fuss,
   Why we drink the health of each high titled beldame;
What's a queen, or a princess, or duchess to us?
   We ne'er have spoke to and seen them but seldom.
Fill a bumber, my host, and I'll give you a toast,
   We all have convers'd with, and ev'ry one knows,
Fill it up to the top, and drink ev'ry drop,
   Here's —— in a bumper wherever she goes!

Your high-sounding titles that kings can create,
   Derive all their lustre and weight from the donor;
But —— can despise all the mockery of state,
   For she's in herself the true fountain of honor;
She fixes for life the rank of a wife,
   In her does the husband his honor repose;

Her titles are bright, all in her own right,
  Here's —— in a bumper wherever she goes!

In rags or brocades, she is equally great,
  Her fountain gives rapture to all that bathe in it!
On a rush-bottom chair, or a down bed of state,
  To bliss we're transported in less than a minute!
She's banished care, as a foe to despair,
  She's the loviliest Lethe to soften her woes;
Nothing nature can boast can rival the toast,
  Of —— in a bumper wherever she goes!

Your wiseacre critics are puzzling their brains,
  How crowns and how coronets first came in fashion;
But one peep at her's would have saved them the pains,
  For —— wore a coronet since the creation;
A title so old, ne'er bartered for gold,
  The whole British peerage would vainly oppose;
Then let mother Eve due homage receive;
  Here's —— in a bumper wherever she goes!

That peers on the trial of peers are to sit,
  Is their greatest distinction beyond all denial;
But —— tho' untitled by patent of writ,
  Can bring, *suo jure* even kings to a trial;

Condemn'd to wear horns, poor G—ve—t scorns,
　The judgment he passes on impotent beaux;
So justly severe may she ever appear,
　Here's —— in a bumper wherever she goes!

That nobles are born the advisers of kings,
　Is a maxim establish'd in every free nation;
Then sure a just claim to that title she brings,
　Whose rhet'ric effected the great reformation;
Tho' Charles lent his ears to his periwig peers,
　Yet —— was the counsellor under the rose;
She whispered her mind—the commons grew kind—
　Here's —— in a bumper wherever she goes!

That nobles are sentenc'd to die by the axe,
　For breach of allegiance—we all must have read is—
Thus —— when the bond of decorum she cracks,
　Like a queen or a princess is always beheaded;
The king without fees will execute these,
　While none but the hangman will meddle with those!
Then since from the throne such deference is shown,
　Here's —— in a bumper wherever she goes!

Your stars and your garters, and ribbons profuse,
  And wide coat of arms that a beggar might quarter;
How faint are their splendour, how trifling their use,
  Compar'd with the star that shines over the garter!
The star in the front is the emblem of ——
  In a lovely field ardent, crown'd sable, she glows,
And two rampant —— as supporters we fix,
  Here's —— in a bumper wherever she goes!

THE BRITISH FAIR.

  I sing the British fair one's charms,
    A theme renown'd in story;
  It well deserves more polish'd lays,
    For 'tis our boast and glory.
When mad-brained lust excitement spreads,
    The fair one is desired,
Nor will she shun the sperm of love,
    But grant whate'er's required.

Then, oh, protect the British fair,
  Be mindful of their merit;
And when that Venus beats to arms,
  They'll show their daring spirit.

When Priapus the fair one fires,
  With love's electric potion,
Oh how she pants, oh how she sighs!
  Each vig'rous nerve's in motion;
Now twisting, twining different ways,
  Each am'rous thought she traces;
But oh, for man, for man she sighs,
  Substantial man's embraces!
      Then, oh, &c.

Behold her on a bed or couch,
  Her beateous thighs extended;
Behold Eve's chasm op'd to your view,
  Unguarded, undefended;
Say, Britons, does a sight like this,
  Not fire and alarm ye?
Oh yes, it arms the rampant boy
  With courage to encharm ye.
      Then, oh, &c.

As thus reclin'd the fair one lies,
  A tempting sight before you,

Oh! how to give her soul delight,
　The wanton will implore you!
With joy she sees undaunted ——
　Nine inches full in measure;
Oh! how her —— now ebbs and flows,
　To squeeze the darling treasure!
　　　Then, oh, &c.

The solar dream of life she guides,
　Into her gaping centre,
And swears 'tis but Anacreon's sons
　Have there a right to enter;
For they are worth beauty's charms,
　Whose pride is to protect them;
Nor from the vale of British ——,
　Will beauty e're reject them.
　　　Then, oh, &c.

BLACK JOCK.

Who has e'er been at Holburn, must needs know the Bell
Where Lucy and Katy, two sisters, do dwell,
　With their black Jocks, and bellies so white.

None ever saw Lucy but wish'd to have kiss'd her,
Yet her charms were eclipsed by those of her sister;
So gay, so easy, so genteel, on my life,
That each was fit for an emperor's wife,
    With their, &c.

With romping fatigued, and the heat of the weather,
One day they lay down on a bed both together,
    With their, &c.
They sigh'd, and talk'd of I do not know what,
Till a little sound sleep put an end to their chat;
I forgot to premise they were stripp'd to the smock,
And the treacherous chamber-door wanted a lock,
    To their black, &c.

Young Cupid, who's ever alert at his post,
Thought the occasion too good to be lost,
    To their, &c.
Away then he slipp'd and return'd in a trice,
With a cock of the game, and a pearl of great price;
Says he, now you see they're both fast asleep,
Slip gently in, and try for a peep,
    At their black, &c.

In then he slipp'd and open'd the latch,
Resolv'd in a critical moment to catch
    Their black, &c.

But oh, as he star'd, when he came to the bed,
In their faces how blended the white and the red;
Such arms, such bubbies, such legs, and such thighs,
But the thing of all things which attracted his eyes,
  Was their black, &c.

Young Lucy he found, lay most opportune,
So he toss'd up her smock, and quickly got in
  To her, &c.
As long as he could he remain'd in the seat,
And the faster he danc'd the sounder she slept,
Till at last he's obliged to beat a retreat,
  From her black, &c.

Next Katy he saw, and her —— to bespatter,
Fresh vigour he found, he swore he'd have at her
  Black Jock, &c.
But in this he had reckon'd without any host,
For he could not get in, her legs were so cross'd,
He tried every means to make matters fit,
But all was in vain, for the never could hit
  Her black, &c.

Enrag'd at the baulk, out his scissors he took,
And out of revenge, he cut off every lock,
  From her black, &c.

SPORTSMEN'S TOASTS.

May the sports of the chase never create lassitude.

May the horns of the buck never disgrace the brows of a sportsman.

May every chase be fairly pursued, especially that of the fair sex.

May neither hurt nor bruise ever restrain the sportsmen's pursuit.

May the death of the game prove a source of health to the sportsman.

Health in our sports, harmony in our cups, and honesty in our loves.

The hen pheasant, that cocks her feathers when she feels the shot.

The cunning hare, that flattens when she sees her pursuer.

May the end of the chase prove the beginning of happiness.

The Suffolk filly, that never threw her rider out of the saddle.

The beagle, that runs by the nose, and not by the sight.

www.ingramcontent.com/pod-product-compliance
Lightning Source LLC
Chambersburg PA
CBHW020103170426
43199CB00009B/375